One-Room
Schoolhouses of
NEW HAMPSHIRE

One-Room Schoolhouses of

Schoolhouses of

NEW HAMPSHIRE

Primers, Penmanship & Potbelly Stoves

BRUCE D. HEALD

Charleston — London

THE
History
PRESS

Published by The History Press
Charleston, SC 29403
www.historypress.net

Front cover, top: Bog School in Campton, New Hampshire. *Photo courtesy of the New Hampshire Historical Society*; *bottom*: Little Red Schoolhouse. *Photo courtesy of Wikimedia Commons, contributor Joscinklin.*
Back cover, bottom: Walpole Academy, Walpole New Hampshire. *Photo courtesy of Library of Congress, Historic American Buildings Survey, 1959.*

First published 2014

Manufactured in the United States

ISBN 978.1.62619.523.3

Library of Congress CIP data applied for.

Notice: The information in this book is true and complete to the best of our knowledge. It is offered without guarantee on the part of the author or The History Press. The author and The History Press disclaim all liability in connection with the use of this book.

Contents

Foreword

Few aspects of New Hampshire history engender as much nostalgia and curiosity as the district schools, which in their heyday numbered in the thousands and were extremely important parts of community life in addition to their primary roles as providers of basic elementary education to the state's young people.

In this work, we find a carefully researched account of how the state and its people struggled to build an educational system that would serve every child, a radical New World idea that, as it spread throughout colonial America, would become a vital element in the eventual success and strength of our democratic society.

Bruce Heald captures both the nuts and bolts of the district school system and the broader cultural and philosophical issues that surrounded the institution as it evolved over nearly three centuries of time. We will recognize many concerns that prevailed long ago in the continual debates that mark educational policymaking at the local and state levels in New Hampshire today.

As the number of people who can count attendance at a one- or two-room district school as part of their life's story continues to decline, this volume affords us a solid record of how these schools came to be, how they functioned and what their enduring legacy is. As a product of New Hampshire district schools, I greatly value this bringing together of facts and data heretofore scattered across the state's landscape.

STEPHEN H. TAYLOR
Meriden, New Hampshire

Acknowledgements

Norman Alkinson; Ashland Historical Society; George Bush; Colbrook Academy; Concord Public School; Lorenca Consuelo; Coos County Teachers' Association; Craydon Village School; Farmington Historical Society; James M. Greenwood; Deborah Herrington; Frank A. Hill, Holderness Historical Society; Roger Kelley; Laconia Historical Society; Lee Historical Society; Littleton Historical Society; Meredith Historical Society; Ruth Moulton; Moultonborough Historical Society; New Hampshire Grange; New Hampshire legislature; North Parsonsfield, Maine Historical Society; Hobart Pillsbury; Plymouth State University; William F. Robinson; Dr. Charles C. Rounds; Sandwich Historical Society; Frank N. Scott; Jonathan Smith; and Stephen Taylor.

Introduction

L earning was widespread in colonial New Hampshire. Colonial New England Protestants used the Bible faithfully in their early education for the preparation of the moral salvation of the youth.

Parents and communities know well that proper formation in the educational development is most essential in preparing sons and daughters for a productive, successful life. Most important was "good citizenship, the proper preparation in the three R's and the general principals of law, commerce, money and government."

Daniel Webster wrote the following regarding childhood education practices in the New World: "For America in her infancy to adopt the maxims of the Old World would be to stamp the wrinkles of old age upon the bloom of youth, and to plant the seed of decay in a vigorous cradle...let the first word he lisps be Washington. The national character is not yet formed."

Historian/author Lorenca Consuelo Rosal presented the state of children's educations when America was first settled: "When the first European settlers arrived in New Hampshire, there were no teachers to instruct their children. Most settlers did not see a need for such instruction. Timbering, fishing, farming, building, sawmilling, candle making, spinning, weaving and sewing were the only skills needed for survival. These skills could be taught at home."

The basic education took place in the district school, which was organized, supervised and financed via local taxation, tuition and what other revenue was available through local and state aid. The district system had become prevalent in New Hampshire during the second half of the eighteenth century. This growth was most apparent as population dispersed outward from towns and outlying neighborhoods demanded control over their schools.

The schools were identified in the local school (town) reports by numbers only, due to the multiplicity of school district numbers, which were assigned to neighborhood schools in each town. The district school was often too small to accommodate the increasing number of scholars who attended during the winter months, when farm work slackened. The location for the district school was most often too small and undesirable. In some instances, old schools in a district were replaced by new buildings, and sometimes, a district formed a union with another town.

Within the one-room grammar school, children's home life diversity—variance in the availability of supplies, parents' support salaries and parents' working conditions—challenged our teachers. Most teachers attempted to group the children into classes based on the level of supplies that were available from home. Thus, each child would bring to school whatever the family happened to have, which were often books that had been passed down by his or her parents.

In the face of these challenges, many teachers did well, but others performed quite poorly. There was no possible way to generalize about the success of teachers in the rural schools of our early Republic. The teacher made memorization the students' major task. The young scholars studied at their desks in preparation for rote recitation in front of the master. Repetitive drilling and a little physical discipline constituted their entire elementary education.

The teachers of the district school were examined in most academic disciplines, as well as other branches that were prescribed by the district school committee or superintending committee; these could possibly include "the study of surveying, algebra, geometry, bookkeeping, philosophy, chemistry, or any of them and other suitable studies." Teachers proposing to teach in such schools were examined in those branches in addition to those required of other supervising teachers.

New Hampshire district schools were closely tied to their communities. Inexpensive and under tight controls, they satisfied communities' desires for elementary education.

The schoolmaster was concerned with discipline and moral character; thus, during the eighteenth and nineteenth centuries, teachers often applied the physical threat of the birch. It was said that this taught morals, and the moral education of children in the district school was the mission of the state. Local school committees ritualistically announced that good discipline made good government, and good government in the schoolroom was a prerequisite of learning. If the scholar was not whipped more than three times a week, he could consider himself most fortunate.

The textbooks lauded liberty but left its direction vague. In 1848, Horace Mann argued that "the common district school should not allow any controversial issues to be taught in the classroom; furthermore, it was considered that the child of depravity in knowledge and virtue is educated in the school of depravity, and what is true of the individual is true of the communities."

For better or worse, our early communities were knit into a network of exchange and communication. This could only foster education and a clear field for new institutional development in a new nation whose Protestant ministers competed for allegiance through the printed pages and the pulpit, while they recommended Bible study for salvation and moral guidance.

The master of the school demanded the scholars to be of good character and morally prepared for his or her place to be filled in life. It was the school that was responsible for mirroring, in general, the traits of the surrounding culture. The role of the school was clear: to make men moral.

In *One-Room Schoolhouses of New Hampshire*, I wish to relate the elementary balance in the common district school; the first schoolhouse, its growth and development; the rural school's problems and its discipline; the pedagogical creed; the teacher's responsibility in the rural school; and the attendees' recollections of the district school in New Hampshire.

Most of the town's people (and hence voters) considered that "the One-room Schools [were] the oxygen of life and learning."

Prelude

L et us reflect back to the beginning of the seventeenth century, when the Renaissance of England was at its height and the upper classes were keenly aware of the intellectual progress of the day. Their educational practices were based on aristocratic notions, and it was considered that schooling was not for the masses but rather for the privileged few. Consequently, the state made little effort to provide free education in all disciplines. The state took little responsibility for educators' support except to require teachers to be licensed by the king and religious leaders. This was to guard against the teaching of heresy and other controversial material. New Hampshire was compelled to follow such teaching while it was under Great Britain's rule.

Despite this influence, the school system in New England became far advanced of that of any other section of America. This was not due to any difference in the character of the people but to the fact that circumstances in New England were more favorable for the establishment of schools. Our people lived in townships where the great majority of residents belonged to the same religious sect. It was, therefore, easier for them to cooperate in founding and maintaining schools than it was in those rural areas in which people were divided into many religious sects.

Attendance was voluntary and many local communities left schooling to the discretion of the family. This caused educational opportunities to be uneven, and training beyond the rudiments was not widespread.

Admittedly, education did play an important role in reconciling freedom and order and was soundly designed to prepare our men and women to become morally trained in order to produce well-behaved citizens.

The founders of our Republic recognized the necessity of properly educating the youth of the land if our country was to endure throughout the forthcoming generations. These same forefathers realized the importance of education. It is a fact that there was no real national educational consciousness until about 1820, forty-four years after New Hampshire became a state. Thaddeus Stevens, who did more toward establishing the public schools than any other individual, spoke in defense of the Pennsylvania educational bill in 1834 before the legislature of that state. In part, he said:

> *If an elective Republic is to endure for any length of time, every elector must have sufficient information not only to accumulate wealth and take care of his pecuniary concerns, but to direct wisely the Legislature, the ambassadors, and the executive of the Nation—for some part of all these things, some agency in approving on disapproving of them falls to every freeman. If, then, the permanency of our Government depends upon such knowledge, it is his duty of the government to see that means of information be diffused to every citizen. This is a sufficient answer to those who deem education a private and not a public duty.*

As changes occurred in our country from the time of President Lincoln, the public school system changed to meet new needs. At that time in history, it became an accepted idea that the proper unit for education should be by the state. In a small way, New Hampshire had adopted this principle as far back as 1847, when John W. Rust was chosen to be the commissioner of education. He served for three years, after which ten commissioners of education were appointed, one for each county. In 1860, New Hampshire changed back to the system of one commissioner of education for the entire state.

It was not until 1919 that a law was passed in the state giving any real centralized state authority over the entire public school system. Since that time, the public had made great strides in public educational work in New Hampshire. Educators had succeeded in equalizing the educational opportunities of the scholar in both the city and rural districts.

Thomas Jefferson told an English friend that "literature is not yet a distinct profession with us. Now and then a strong mind arises, and at its intervals from business emits a flash of light."

Daniel Webster, one of New Hampshire's most illustrious sons, must have had education in mind when he wrote, "If we work upon marble, it will perish; if we work on brass, time will efface it; if we rear temples, they will crumble into dust; but if we work upon immortal minds, if we imbue them with principles, with the just fear of God and love of fellowmen, we engrave on those tablets something which will brighten to all eternity."

1

Early History of
New Hampshire Education

During the early colonial days, the Commonwealth of Massachusetts undertook the leadership of education for all New England. A school had been established in the town of Boston by 1635 (Boston Latin School on School Street), and by 1642, a law had been passed by the general court providing that all parents should have their children taught how to read and apply a trade. The Massachusetts law went further "to make primary education compulsory for all parents, where the latter only require the teaching of a trade to the poor child."

The act of 1642, according to the state legislature, aimed to get the most out of children's education. Writing the education system into law protected against parents and schoolmasters who might be too indulgent, distracted or negligent to properly prepare their children for citizenship. The law ordered that communities make sure their children learned to read English in order to learn the laws of the nation and the Bible. It was the intention of the act of 1642 to emphasize good education for the scholars of each district and so provide appropriate benefit to the commonwealth of the Massachusetts Bay Colony.

It was also ordered by the commonwealth that the selectmen in each town have vigilant control over each school district. Parents were not to allow any barbarism in the community, and families had to teach scholars enough to speak the English language and properly receive the capital knowledge and laws, with a penalty of twenty shillings for neglecting their duties. Finally, that catechism of the principles of religion had to be instructed by the master to the children.

Abandoned schoolhouse located near the swamp flood zone. *Courtesy of William F. Robinson.*

The early laws of education passed by the general court were insufficient and weak, and in most cases, these laws were never really attained, though schools were established in a number of towns throughout New England. In the majority of the school districts, the only subjects taught were reading, writing, arithmetic and religious training. Later, this will be illustrated in our first established schools (see Chapter Two).

According to the New Hampshire General Court and its authority, it was the desire for the following to be enforced:

The formation of early education may not be buried in the grave of our forefathers in church and commonwealth, the Lord assisting our endeavors.

Every township within this jurisdiction, after that the Lord hath increased them to the number of fifty householders, shall then forthwith appointe one within theire towne, to teach all such children as shall resort to him, to write and read; whose wages shall be paid either by the parents or masters of such children, or by the inhabitants in general, by way of supplye, as the major parte of those who order the prudential of the towne shall appointe: provided, that those who send their children, bee not oppressed by paying much more than can have them taught for in other townes.

It was further ordered, that where any towne shall increase the number of one hundred families or householders, they shall sett up a grammar schoole, the masters thereof, being able to instruct youths so far as they may bee fitted for the university: and if the town neglects the performance hereof, above one yeare, then every such towne shall pay five pounds per annum, for the next such schoole, till they shall performed this order.

In the town records of Dover, New Hampshire, it was noted that in August 1656, at the town meeting, a gentleman by the name of Charles Buckher chose to vote for a schoolmaster for the town. In 1658, it was agreed by the selectmen together with the town that "twenty-pounds per annum shall be yearly raysed for the Mayntenance of a school-master in the Town of Dover." His duties were to teach all the children in the town. The new schoolmaster would also teach disciplines required by the parents.

It was recommended by the townships that money be raised for this purpose: "One peck of corn or twelve pence was the money or other commodity, of every family, so that the colleges may have some considerable yearly help towards their occasions."

All of the New Hampshire towns did not take kindly to the compulsory laws in regard to the keeping of the common district school, which were established by the general court of Massachusetts. Some individuals in many towns of New Hampshire refused to pay their school taxes except by process of law.

During this time (between 1679 and 1692), New Hampshire separated from the bay state of Massachusetts and then was reunited by petition of the citizens. Besides actions made by the Crown, little was done for education.

It is a fact that out of 374 signers of a petition presented to the court of the Massachusetts Bay Colony in 1600 for protection again the Native Americans, nearly 25 percent were obliged to make their marks, which would indicate a lack, rather than an abundance, of educational privileges.

The time came when the germs of education were strongly implanted in the majority of the New Hampshire citizens. During the first year after New Hampshire's separation from the Bay Colony (1693), when the people were suffering from poverty and enduring hardships of the King William's War, the following ordinance given by the Crown was enforced on the inhabitants:

It is enacted that for the building and repairing of meeting houses, minister's houses, schoolhouses, and allowing a salary to a school master in each town within the Province, the selectmen, in respective towns, shall raise money by an equal rate and assessment upon the inhabitants—and every town within the Province shall from and after the publication hereof, provide a schoolmaster for the supply of the town, on penalty of ten pounds; and for neglect thereof, to be paid, one half to their majesties, and the other half to the poor of the town.

Other laws regarding maintenance of the common school were enacted in 1714, 1719 and 1721, which remained on the books until the adoption of the state constitution in 1784. Selectmen who were derelict in their responsibilities according to their laws were made liable upon their personal estate for the penalty affixed on the towns.

In some of the frontier towns in the state, the law relating to grammar schools was considered a hardship, especially for the selectmen, and there are several instances on record where petitions were granted excusing these newly settled parishes from the grammar school conditions; however, in no instance was any town or parish excused from keeping a school for reading and writing "to which all towns of fifty families were obliged."

Townships soon spread throughout New Hampshire, with citizens being intelligent and deeply religious and soon acquiring no small influence in the affairs of the province. It was assumed that undoubtedly these local citizens were responsible for the enforcement of the school laws and that such stringent provisions were enacted, as were stated in the law of 1721.

In George Bush's essay on the "History of New Hampshire Education," he relates:

> *Between 1680 and 1783 grants of land were made of the incorporated towns for the support of schools. It seems probable that in all the grants made by the Masonian proprietors, by the Massachusetts Colony, and John Wentworth; one lot or share was reserved in each town for a school. But this cannot be said of all the numerous grants made by our trusty and well-behaved Benning Wentworth, esq., Governor and Commander-in-Chief of the Province of New Hampshire. He even refused to charter a college or the petition of a convention of ministers, presented in 1758, who desired the government and religion by laying a foundation for the best instruction of youth. But in 1769, under the administration of Governor John Wentworth, the charter was secured, the college [Dartmouth] founded and a grant of 44,000 acres was made for it.*

Jeremy Belknap, who was considered to be the first historian of New Hampshire, recommended that the selectmen of the town be prepared to make wise decisions, thus providing the means and ability to instruct the students in proper order. Those in power, however, did not necessarily have

A typical turn-of-the-century abandoned schoolhouse at the crossroads in the country. *Courtesy of A. Ferguson.*

the students' best interests at heart. Most historians during the 1800s agreed that "the proper understanding of literature is a danger to unprincipled men, as it may expose them to contempt." The neglect of schools was among evidence of the time period's sad prostration of morals. Jeremy Belknap also maintained that "it affords a melancholy prospect to the friends of science and of virtue and excited some generous and philanthropic persons to devise other methods of education."

In the compact of September 5, 1792, many educators found the following as the basis of all future legislation concerning education in New Hampshire:

> *Knowledge and learning, generally diffused through a community being essential to the preservation of a free government and spreading the opportunities and advantages of education through the various parts of the country being highly conducive to promote this end, it shall be the duty of the legislators and magistrates in all future periods of government, to cherish the interest of literature of the sciences, and all seminaries and public schools; to encourage public and private instruction, rewards and immunities for the promotion of agriculture, arts, sciences, commerce, manufacture, and natural history of the country.*

2

School Districts Established

B y 1805, the school districts were established. An act by the New
Hampshire legislature empowered towns to divide into school districts
and gave each district a right to raise money by tax for the purpose of erecting,
repairing or purchasing a schoolhouse and for securing all necessary supplies
for the same. All qualified town voters were authorized to vote in district
affairs. The establishment of school districts was a large step in the right
direction. But districts multiplied by a far greater extent than expected. The
sheer numbers of new schools in small districts throughout the state led to
abuse and problems with the school systems.

Colonial farmers had strongly complained that although they were taxed
for the upkeep of the village school, the distance to it often made attendance
a hardship. From this problem grew the concept of the district country
school, which appeared in the 1800s. It was to the credit of the majority
of the New Hampshire people, however, that in spite of this opposition—
some of which was, and is still, to be found in all communities—public
schools were to be maintained. It should be noted that due to poor roads,
the districts were quite small and the institutions known as neighborhood
or family schools.

By 1808, an act from the New Hampshire state legislature was passed that
enlarged the range of instruction in the common schools and that expanded
taxes to be used for schools.

In addition to the skills of instruction (noted in the Introduction), the
schoolmaster was required to provide a certificate of good moral character

This certifies that Miss Huldah Jane Leavitt is, in our opinion well qualified to teach any of the branches required by the laws of the State, to be taught in our common schools. She has been a successful teacher, and is of good moral character, and worthy the esteem and confidence of any one wishing to employ her; and with pleasure we commend her to those in search of a teacher.

Charles Burnham) Superin-
O. Butler   ) tending
) Committee

Meredith Nov. 6th 1863.

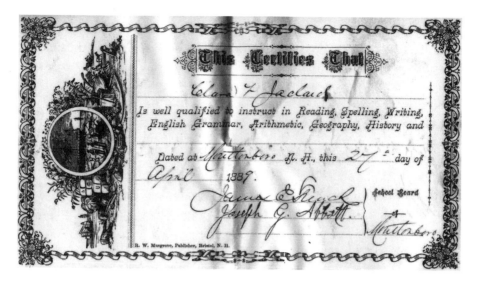

Above: "This Certifies That Clara L. Jaclaid is well qualified to instruct in Reading, Spelling, Writing, English, Grammar, Arithmetic, Geography, History and—." Dated April 27, 1889. *Courtesy of the Moultonborough Historical Society.*

Opposite, top: The Waldron Schoolhouse on the Bay Road in Farmington, New Hampshire, was typical of the school building in outlying areas after the town was divided into sixteen school districts in 1805. Note the privy located to the right of the school. *Courtesy of the author.*

Opposite, bottom: "This letter certifies that Miss Huluah Jane Leavitt is in our opinion well qualified to teach any of the branches required by the law of the State, to be taught in our common schools. She has been a successful teacher, and is of good moral character, and worthy the esteem and confidence of anyone wishing to employ her, and with pleasure we recommend her to those in search of a teacher, Meredith Nov. 8 1863. Charles Burnham Superintending Committee." *Courtesy of the Meredith Historical Society, New Hampshire.*

from the selectmen or minister of the town in which he resided. It was the duty of the town to appoint a committee of three or more persons, whose duty it was to visit and inspect the school annually in its respective town or parish in "a manner which might judge most conducive to the progress of literature, morality and religion." This was certainly a new feature in school legislation and may have suggested a trend toward a superintending committee. The exact status of the town superintending committee was difficult to define. From 1827 until 1848, its duties ranged from having entire control of the schools to being merely an advisory body. In 1859, a bill was passed somewhat enlarging the duties of the superintending committee, although in all important points, it was identical with the law of 1827. It was to select and dismiss teachers, prescribe rules of conduct for the pupils and decide which textbooks should be used and the courses of study to be followed. Each teacher was to be supplied with a register, and the committee was obliged, at the end of the year, to summarize and return to the state officer certain statistics from the same. This law was later repealed in 1885.

In 1865, the state had 2,299 school districts, this being close to the maximum number that had existed shortly before the Civil War. Five years later, in 1870, the state legislature passed a law that "any town may, at any time abolish the school district therein, and shall there upon forthwith take possession of all the school houses, land, apparatus, and other property owned and (or) used for school purposes."

This movement began the decline of district domination and support in New Hampshire public schools. By 1880, the district units numbered 2,010. It was not until 1899 that the beginning of a new type of educational administration in the public school system, which was called the "Supervisory Union," arose. And it was in 1909 that the New Hampshire General Court passed the initial legislation authorizing state aid to create supervisory unions, apportioned on the basis of equalized tax evaluation. It is worth mentioning that in 1899 the legislature passed the Grange School Law, which provided $25,000 for one-room schools. At one point, the temperance union convinced the legislature to include studying the effects of alcohol. In 1907, the Grange, a farmers' association, created the position of a superintendent and committee to oversee the schools. This committee was to be known as the Prudential Committee and was required to apprise the local residents qualified to vote in district affairs of any meeting of the school district and business to be acted on at the meeting:

The district could confer no authority except at a legal meeting but may, at said meeting, upon sufficient warrant, ratify and confirm the proceeding of a previous meeting. It was also agreed by the committee that the new Hampshire Common School was the source of the state's greatness and success, and the earlier we wake up to the realization of this fact, the better it will be for the State of New Hampshire.

Such warrant be served by the posting a copy thereof, attested by the committee, at the door of the schoolhouse if there be any at the district, otherwise at one or more public places in the district, fourteen days, at least, prior to the day of the meeting.

To the pride of our state, this is only one of the hundreds of old one-room schools that now stand idle across our landscape. This one is in the town of Goffstown. *Courtesy of William F. Robinson.*

During the early 1800s, the population had begun to separate into manufacturing cities and villages; hence, the population became more equally distributed over the territory. The economy had kept down the number of teachers, and so the schools were overcrowded. Many parents thought that public interest had been weakened because of the reduced number of districts.

The number of school districts was reduced to 275 in 1890. Under this system, 679 fewer teachers had been employed.

In the year 1885, the length of the school year was 19.95 weeks. Three years later, it had increased to 22.90 weeks, and in 1890, it was 23.95 weeks.

According to the State Superintendent's Report for 1870: "One half the schools in the state average less than 12 scholars; the average, including city and village schools, was only 18 scholars. The average attendance of pupils was only two-thirds the total number; that is, one-third of the school money was absolutely thrown away in consequence of the number in attendance."

The following is a report of school statistics taken from the State Superintendent's Report for 1850:

Number of school districts	*2,167*
Number of pupils above 4 years of age attending	
two weeks or more	*78,863*
Number attending the winter schools	*77,806*
Number attending summer school	*61,498*
Average length of the winter schools (in weeks)	*9.45*
Average length of summer schools (in weeks)	*9.25*
Average monthly wages of male teachers	
(exclusive of board)	*$14.73*
Average monthly wages for female teachers	
(exclusive of board)	*$6.21*
Number of male teachers employed	
in winter schools	*1,246*
Number of female teachers employed	
in winter schools	*961*
Amount raised by taxation for schools	*$145,892.12*

COMMON DISTRICT SCHOOL STATISTICS, 1890

Number of schools	*2,302*
Average length of schools (in weeks)	*23.55*
Number of pupils enrolled	*59,813*
Average attendance	*41,526*
Number of male teachers	*306*
Number of female teachers	*2,808*
Average monthly wages paid male teachers	*$45.88*
Average monthly wages paid female wages	*$25.64*
Number of school houses	*2,078*
Amount raised for schools by town taxes	*$515,141.63*
Amount raises for schools by district taxes	*$144,434.10*

The following account was recorded by historian Lorenca Consuelo Rosal's *God Save the People*:

In 1850, New Hampshire was proud to be one of only two states in which 98% of the residents could read. However, by 1917 test results were much different. During the First World War, new machines such as the airplane and tank were first used on the battlefield. Factories were called upon to provide technical equipment for the war effort. Well-trained doctors and nurses were needed to serve in field hospitals. The war could not be won without the efforts of a skilled and educated population.

The United States government developed tests to see if a recruit was able to serve in a modern army. A large number of New Hampshire recruits did poorly on these tests. Many citizens felt the school system was to blame. The Great School Law was also a result of Progressives' criticism of child labor, which had prevented many children from receiving an education.

The Great School Law of 1919 created a State Board of Education to make rules and regulations to be followed in every town in the state. Minimum standards of school quality were established. The law also required that all classes be taught in English, that children attend school for a minimum number of years and that the state give certain financial aid to schools. The town districts, however, were still to provide a large share of the funds needed to operate local schools. Importantly, the law also divided the state into School Supervisory Unions, which today are called School Administrative Units or (SAU) At one time, SAU's were organized along railroad lines, so that the superintendent could travel easily from district to district.

Some people objected to the Great School Law of 1919. They said that since the Board of Education could make rules that were to apply across the state, the New Hampshire tradition of home rule (local control) had been lost. However, others argued that the Board of Education could adopt flexible rules which towns could apply as best fit their situations.

As New Hampshire's economic base changed from agriculture to mill industry high tech, the state's educational aid had changed too. Today the purpose of education is no longer solely to train students to understand the Bible and the laws, as was true in the 1640's. Education is now geared towards providing for all sorts of community needs. In the 1960's and 1970's for example, the need for skilled technicians in the computer field increased.

Rosal also records that school district are organized in two ways:

1. The Cooperative System—Instead of each district using tax funds to support several schools, the districts pool their resources. Wealthier and poorer towns work together to support a larger uniform school by the cooperative program, the number of districts in the state is reduced and management costs are lowered.

The cooperative district may even cross borders. For example may be Norwich, Vermont and Hanover, New Hampshire, have cooperated for the mutual good of the students. Sometimes cooperatives are formed to provide a joint high school, grammar school or both.

2. The Area Program—This program is similar to the cooperative, but the old districts remain in existence. Neighboring districts may find an appropriately located town and send their children to school here. The district, which received these children is called the receiving district. The other is called sending district. The sending district pays tuition to the receiving district for each sending district pupil which attend[s] the AREA school. The tax money needed to pay the tuition is smaller than what is needed to support a small town school. Therefore, while the AREA program does not reduce the number of the districts, it does advance equality of education, by enabling wealthy and needy towns to act as one.

FINANCING THE DISTRICT SCHOOL

According to Master Dudley Leavitt, the average monthly wages during the 1800s were approximately six dollars a month, and sometimes they ran as low as four dollars a month. Quite often, the master of the district school was not paid in money at all but drew his salary in so many bushels of grain, wheat or rye.

The town of Bath, New Hampshire, voted one year to raise sixty bushels of wheat for the support of the school. In fact, this item of raising grain to be used for school purposes is frequently met with in the town's records. The use of grain for money at times when coin was very scarce or when the country was overrun with paper money and its value considered to be almost nothing was common. Good grain could always be exchanged for the necessities of life, and its value as a medium of exchange was more or less a fixed value.

The two following receipts not only show instances of this kind of payment but also indicate the relative value placed on the master's teaching as compared with that of the "marn's" (female) teaching.

March 21, 1792

Then my son Robert Hogg, received seventeen bushels of Rye from Simon Kezar of the Town of Sutton, which was due to me for teaching schooling two months in Sutton.
Per me,

Robert Hogg

Methuen, Feb. 1, 1791

Received of Jacob Marston and Hezekiah Parker six bushels of Rye, it being in full for my keeping school for them and others last six months. Lydia Parker.

It should not be assumed that this was the entire money the teacher lived on during the year. The schools were generally so arranged in the different neighborhoods that they would begin one after another. The master could compensate by moving from one district to the next and be constantly supplied with a school.

In addition to the funds raised directly for the support of the district schools, there was usually a small revenue from the "town lot." In all grants of township made by the Masonian Proprietors, by Massachusetts and by John Wentworth II, one lot or share, generally about one hundred acres of the land, was set aside for the use of schools. This was usually accomplished via other state governors. Other towns appropriated the land for public purposes and occasionally the lot was sold. On March 12, 1749, the town of Rochester "voted that the selectmen of this town let out the school lot to those that will give the most for it for the present year; the rent to be combated to the towns."

The school had two sessions a year: one in summer, which operated from eight to ten weeks, and one in the winter, from ten to twelve weeks. The summer school teacher was paid $6.00 per month and board; this averaged to $1.25 per week. The winter teacher received from $18.00 to $22.00 per month and board. The summer school was of the primary grade, for all children old enough to work were kept employed at home. During the winter, the pupils varied in age from four to twenty-one years.

Besides the methods above mentioned for raising school money, in the very earliest schools it was the custom "that every man should bring two feet of wood for each scholar that he sent to school" and "that every man should chop his own wood that he brings to the schoolhouse."

Later, however, this particular custom changed, and the task of furnishing the school firewood was generally set up at auction and struck off to the lowest bidder. It was sometimes bid on by a man who had a quantity of cheap wood that he wished to get rid of and who accordingly determined to dispose of it at schools for the boys to work up. Finally, on one occasion, when there were three more days before the school would close, a generous member of the town drew a cord of ash and said that it must last for the rest of the school term. The older boys determined they would not be dictated to on the quantity of wood. The pitch fried out the pine knots in the ceiling, but at sundown, not a stich of wood remained. The owner was obliged to haul another load to the school.

The Dame School

The dame schools were usually taught in the summer and were for the smaller children and the girls. The boys at this time were getting in the hay and assisting their fathers. The women who had charge of the summer schools were expected to teach the girls sewing and knitting as well as spelling and reading. Arithmetic was considered entirely superfluous for girls and, in fact, was seldom taught even in the winter schools. Frequently, the unmarried women who taught these "marm" (female teacher) schools earned something more than their school wages by spinning between school terms for the family with whom they boarded. They sometimes earned as much as fifty cents per week by this means. Many of the teachers rotated from place to place throughout the township.

The old schoolhouse on Bean Road near Sibley Road, circa 1890. *Courtesy of Moultonborough Historical Society, photo by Roger Kelly.*

THE EARLY SCHOOLHOUSES

There has been a great deal of nostalgia concerning the old-time district school, where the academics were well taught to the rhythm of the hick'ry stick, and certainly at its best, the district school had something to command it.

The very early schoolhouses were not painted red; they were log or clapboard. They were often not in ideal locations. Cleared land was scarce and was usually located on property that was swampy and unworthy for a schoolhouse. The schoolhouse needed only to be built in exactly the center of the district, often landing it in less-than-ideal locations. Certainly many of the school officials bemoaned the poor location of the house, claiming that it demonstrated public indifference to the youth's education. Schoolhouses were sometimes adjacent to the cooper's shop or between a blacksmith's shop and a sawmill.

The district school was often too small to accommodate the increasing number of scholars who attended during the winter months, when farm

Above: Interior of the Blazo School, North Parsonsfield's, Maine, one-room schoolhouse. *Courtesy of the North Parsonsfield Historical Society.*

Opposite, top: The interior of the Moultonborough school as seen today. *Courtesy of Moultonborough Historical Society, photo by Norman Alkinson.*

Opposite, bottom: The one-room school in Farmington, New Hampshire. Teacher Floss Locke stands with her class in front of the Ten Rod Road School in 1911. *Courtesy of the Farmington Historical Society.*

work slackened. The structure was usually one story high and about twenty by thirty feet, costing perhaps $400. Up to sixty young scholars would often spend six-hour days in a space for less than thirty.

The usual plan included built-in desks with benches on which the older scholars could face the master or the center of the room. In the front were benches for the younger children, generally close to the stove or fireplace. Beyond those benches were the plain pine desk for the teacher and two small chairs. The teacher's desk was placed on a low platform, positioned in front, depending on the location of the stove. The unpainted room was most inadequate for learning. There was little space, lack of furniture, little learning material and windows without curtains or shutters.

Come winter, the proximity of one's schoolmates was welcome, as body heat offered the best warmth in the drafty buildings. Even though each school had a fireplace or stove, it only served to bake the children who were located near the stove, while those who sat farthest away froze.

The typical potbellied stove found in the rural schoolhouse. This is the interior of the Moultonborough school as seen today. *Courtesy of the Moultonborough Historical Society, photo by Norman Alkinson.*

Illness often shut down the school. Tuberculosis could possibly take the lives of members of an entire school.

A more detailed and interesting description of the early schools in Littleton was painted by an unknown author:

The desks, if we examine them, will have, hollowed out upon their upper side, course images of Indian fights, canal boats, tomahawks, fox and geese and checker boards, miniature river systems, and many a cut and hack, made in the mere exuberance of youthful spirits, without any apparent design. A look at the walls reveals to us the stucco work of spit-balls, fired at flies or imaginary targets, by mischievous boys, and places, too, bare plaster and whitewash, where some ball or ink bottle has struck in the absence of the teacher.

The following description of an early school in New Hampshire has been taken from Samuel Willey's (1766–1826) *Incidents in the White Mountain History.* This brief article was reprinted by Ernest E. Bisbee in 1938:

It was kept by a veteran teacher, peculiar in his habits and aspect, keen, fearless and practiced in his business. He kept a house we shall not describe at great length. In a few words, it was contracted in its dimensions, uninviting in its general appearance, and open on its wall and floor, so that both the light and winds of Heaven could pass freely through it. Under the house the hogs had as free access as the light and winds had into it above. This was their cherished place of resort; and they were there, too, every day, as regularly as the scholars were to the school. They greatly annoyed the teacher, but were as acceptable to most of the scholars, as they were troublesome to him. Many were the scenes of amusement, during that school, which took place with these hogs.

Sometimes, after lying and rolling on the ground awhile, grunting and growling as they rooted each other's sides, they would rise up, and, brushing along under the floor, carry their bristles up through the large cracks into plain sight of the scholars.

Seeing these one of them would creep along, when the master's eyes were turned, and give them a sharp pull. Then immediately would come squeal, and after that sharp words from the teacher.

"Boys, let those hogs alone, mind your studies."

For a moment they would put their faces into their books and seem content, but they wouldn't stay put. Presently, the bristles would be seen

On the first day, students wait for their teacher. *Courtesy of the author.*

moving along the cracks of the floor again, and they would follow another pull, and then immediately another squeal would become stronger, sterner words from the teacher.

"Boys I say, let those hogs alone. If you don't, I'll give it to you."

This might stop them for a while. But the itching in them for fun was not allayed. Their fingers worked nervously to behold of the bristles again, and provoke another squeal. Now things became more serious, and the teacher must put more authority and power into his words, so he said, "Consumption boys"—that was the word he often used—"Consumption, boys! What do you mean? If you don't let those hogs along I'll tan your jackets for you! I'll make your backs smoke!"

Many early schools preserved and rebuilt these structures with walls showing old pictures, and numerous memories have been related to the visitors. On July 4, 1947, the Locke Haven School at Crystal Lake near Enfield reopened the school. And a friendly unknown historian observed:

> How few can recall the dunce stool and the humiliating dunce cap...the traditional pictures of Lincoln and Washington above the teacher's head... wood-bound states with squeaky, flint-like chalk...the "central heating system"—an iron stove, surrounded, in snow season with a variety of steaming boots and galoshes—the splintery pine board floor from which the student could wiggle his desk loose with two days' careful effort—if he were not caught...those battle-scarred desks, grooved and etched by older brothers or even fathers (but never sisters or mothers!).
>
> And the school marm—despite her hickory sidearm, she was an endearing soul, a combination of pedant, administrator, truant officer, janitor, and guidance department...In her undiversified state she was often able to give a personal touch to the lives of her charges—an element that seems somehow lost in modern education, for all its undeniable worth.

According to historian Stephen Taylor's statements, which appeared in the *New Hampshire Magazine* in September 2013:

> The schools were valued because they were local. People knew all the parents and the children. You'd have schools on the mountainside that might only keep school for five or six weeks a year, but other schools in the village might keep school for 30. The curriculum, though, was surprisingly fairly uniform with grammar, penmanship, history and arithmetic.
>
> The sentiment and impulse is very strong and continuous just as it was a century ago. They could easily close the doors and ship the children elsewhere for school, but they value the local school thing.
>
> These one-room school houses may be closed for class, but various historical societies have preserved them for visitors, namely:

North School
Kensington, 1842–1952

Indian Stream Historical School House
Pittsburg, 1897–1939

First-day portrait of the class and teachers, 1900s. *Courtesy of the Meredith Historical Society.*

Madison Corner School
Madison, 1835–1949

District Schoolhouse No. 1
Hooksett, 1839–1912

Brick Schoolhouse
Sharon, 1833–1920

District No. 5 School
E. Washington, 1849–1937

District No. 1 Schoolhouse
Nashua, 1841–1921

3

The First Schoolmaster

It was the responsibility of the parents to supply the books and other school material for the students to use. There were sometimes as many different textbooks in use in the school as there were children in attendance. In many instances, the more advanced pupils were allowed to bring from home any reader or book that they might wish to use to further their education. The older scholars sat on benches in the back part of the room and read aloud one after another; the teacher, in the meantime, pretended to listen, but for children having no book, the exercise was tiresome in the extreme and the criticism usually lacking.

An interesting account of this kind of exercise was given by Miss Deane Rankin of Littleton, New Hampshire:

> *The monotony of such a dull exercise often threw our master into a profound slumber, and I remember, one time, I, and another mischievous girl, tried to see how hard we could punch our sleeping pedagogue without awaking him. He was so moderate in returning to consciousness that we had ample time to return to our books with the most intense application, leaving him in entire ignorance as to where the ones were who would presume to disturb his pleasant dreams.*
>
> *It was also the responsibility of the teacher to mend pens for one class, which would be sitting idle, hearing another spell, calling a covey of boys to be quiet, who had nothing to do but make mischief, watch an older scholar, who had been placed standing on a bench in the middle of the room*

for punishment, and to many little ones, passionately answering question of—"may I go out?" "May I go home?" "Tell Johnny to be quiet."

Opening the class usually consisted of an opening exercise of prayer and a salute to the flag. The religious exercises consisted of the students each reading a verse from the Bible and a prayer, which was often very long, by the teacher. It was regularly emphasized that good morals were also an important part of the curriculum, and instruction was faithfully provided by the teacher on all occasions. Truthfulness and honesty were especially emphasized. I do not believe that instruction was provided in patriotism or in the duties of responsibility of citizenship.

The ladder of learning began with the parsing book—the art of reading. During the day's schedule of the curriculum, the teacher attempted to develop reading skills with the students. Students struggled to retain information when they heard too much too quickly, without a chance to retain each piece of information.

Above: Kept in at recess to make up their work. *Courtesy of the author, taken from an old print.*

Opposite: An artistic view of the interior of the old-fashioned school. Many men and women got their starts in such a school, and the pupils were well taught by the master at his desk. *Courtesy of National Life Insurance Co., Montpelier, Vermont.*

SYNOPSIS OF GRAMMATICAL RELATIONS.

See Gram. §§ 35, 36, 37, 28, 34, or Parsing Book, pages 5, 6.

SUBJECT.	MODIFIERS OF THE SUBJECT.	PREDICATE.	MODIFIERS OF THE PREDICATE.
The SUBJECT of a sentence may be a noun or pronoun; a verb in the infinitive; a clause; or any word or letter of which something can be affirmed.	The MODIFIERS of the subject may be a noun in apposition; an adjective, a preposition with its object (adjunct); a participle; a verb in the infinitive; a relative clause; and rarely an adverb.	The PREDICATE of a sentence may be a verb; or the verb be with any word or expression connected with it, to complete an assertion.	The MODIFIERS of the predicate may be a noun in the objective case, (if the verb is transitive;) a verb in the infinitive; an adverb; a preposition with its object (adjunct); a clause; and rarely an adjective.

The Subject, whose meaning is modified by one or more words, is called the MODIFIED (or logical) SUBJECT.

The Predicate, whose meaning is modified by one or more words, is called the MODIFIED (or logical) PREDICATE.

SIMPLE SENTENCES.

MODIFIED SUBJECTS.		MODIFIED PREDICATES.	
SUBJECT.	MODIFIERS OF THE SUBJECT.	PREDICATE.	MODIFIERS OF THE PRED.
Ferdinand,	the king,	held	a council at Cordova.
He,	the marquis of Cadiz,	beheld	from a distance, the peril of the king.
To die	in peace,	is the privilege	of the good.
That you have wronged me	by your denial,	is evident	from your own admission
Evergreens	only, among the trees,	look	verdant, in the winter.
An,	called an article,	is derived	from a Saxon word.
The rose,	so fair and beautiful to-day,	may wither and fade	to-morrow.
Those.	who are obliging,	may expect	to be accommodated.

"Synopsis of Grammatical Relations." Taken from the 1856 *Parsing Book* by Allen H. Weld. *Courtesy of the author.*

The students' first reading book was the Perry's *Reading Book*, which contained limited fables, tales and poetry.

The advanced reading books were filled with extracts from the great speeches of the masters of politics—i.e., Webster, Adams, Hamilton, Jefferson and other men of letters—which expounded on the great deeds of the Revolutionary fathers and the glory of our country. Students were expected to read quickly and loudly with a mind to punctuation. The Bible, particularly the New Testament from the King James Version, was read twice a day for all classes.

Next was the spelling lesson, which was entirely oral and usually conducted by choosing sides and spelling down the line of students. The best speller in the school was a noted personage, and in choosing sides, he was always the first to be called. Sometimes, school districts would unite for a spelling match, and great glory awaited the boy or girl who brought honor to his or her district school.

The spelling words were always done by syllable; each syllable was spelled and pronounced, and then the next syllable was spelled and pronounced. Then both were pronounced together, and the same method was followed throughout the word. When a word like *Constantinople* was spelled in this way, it took considerable time.

According to historian J. Orville Taylor, the students learned to spell using Perry's *Spelling Book*. Even though spelling was one of the most direct lessons the students received, it was also one of the driest. Schoolchildren cared little for how letters were arranged to form words, but they did care whether they were at the head of the class.

For the upper grades, the importance of grammar usage was most crucial, particularly for editing purposes. Taylor noted that punctuation was mostly an art of pointing, leading the reader to pauses and determining the reader's cadence.

Two other references were often used in the early schools of the nineteenth century. One was Master Dudley Leavitt's *Complete Directions for Parsing the English Language* published by Jacob B. Moore in 1826, which givers further insight into the grammar used at the time. Further details of this text may be found in Chapter Four. The other was Allen H. Weld's *Parsing Book*.

According to Weld's preface:

> *The selections which compose the body of the following work are so arranged as to constitute a gradual course of Exercises in* Analyzing *and* Parsing.
>
> *The Rules of Syntax are taken from* WELD'S ENGLISH GRAMMAR *by permission of the Publishers, and to these* rules, *and also to the Grammar from which they are taken, references are occasionally made, to assist the learner in explaining idiomatic or difficult passages.*
>
> *As the extracts are from some of the most accomplished and approved writers, the Ornaments of Style, Figures of Rhetoric, and Scanning, may be profitably attended to by advanced classes.*
>
> *The book may be used by learners in almost any stage of attainment after the elementary principles of Grammar are understood. The work is designed to take the place of Pope's Essay, Thomson's Seasons, Young's Night Thoughts, and other entire poems, which are used as* parsing books *in schools. A variety in the selections, it is believed, will be more profitable and interesting to the learner than any single work can be, which exhibits no gradation in style, and the peculiarities of one writer only.*
>
> *A.H.W.*

It was imperative that the upper grades understand the complete rules of syntax. The rules are provided in Allen H. Weld's *Parsing Book*:

1. Syntax treats of sentences, and teaches the proper construction of words in forming them.

Classification of Sentences

Sentences are of four kinds, declaratory, imperative, interrogative *and* conditional.

A declaratory sentence *is one in which anything is simply affirmed or denied of a subject; as, Time flies; he will not understand a declaration.*

An imperative sentence *is one which expresses a command, an unavoidable fact.*

An interrogative sentence *presents itself as a question…*

Sentences are either simple *or* compound. A simple sentence *consists of but one proposition; a compound sentence consists of two or more simple sentences.*

The simple propositions which make up a compound sentence, are called clauses *or* members.

The leading clause *is one on which the other members depend.*

A dependent clause *is one which makes complete sense only in connection with another clause.*

A similar list of rules for grammatical compositions was written by Dudley Leavitt and published in 1811. This list may be found in Chapter Four entitled "Master Dudley Leavitt."

Regularly, the reading and spelling lessons were followed by the arithmetic lesson taught by the teacher orally—by rote, as it was called. Usually the rules were written out on pieces of birch bark—or on scraps of paper if any pupil was so fortunate as to possess them—and then memorized. Master Leavitt also wrote the *Scholar's Review and Teacher's Daily Assistant*, which was also used for the district school. Chapter Four also elaborates on this mathematical directory for the instructional use of mathematics.

After the arithmetic lesson came recess, and it is needless to say that the decorum of the boys on their entrance to school was not maintained on their exit at recess time or lunch. If a hot lunch were to be available, a family would be assigned to prepare and serve the food. Students would eat what was in the pot, which was kept warm on the stove; however, each student had to provide his or her own bowl and spoon. The teacher would make sure that their bowls were empty before the students were excused for the playground.

It must be remembered that the principle attraction of going to school was the opportunity for youthful social amusement. The rural schools were scattered several miles apart, and the students did not exchange social sport

The Cram School, West Center Harbor. Seen here are (back row, from left to right) teacher Delia Kelly, Blanch Boynton, Mary Webster, Edgar Davis, Hazel Davis, Leon Hawkins, Lavinia Lovett and May Bartlett; (front row, from left to right) Paul H. Perkins, Edward Webster, Leon M. Huntress and Otis Hawkins. *Courtesy of the Center Harbor Historical Society.*

A schoolyard game of tag. *Courtesy of the author.*

activities as compared to those in the village. Thus, the students considered the schools as one long series of holidays.

According to historian J. Orville Taylor:

> *The sports of those early days, indulged in at recess and at noon intermission, were not so very different from those of the children of today. As one of the early chroniclers has put it: "They had pizengool" or goal, tag, snap the whip, high-spy, "eny, meny, miny, mo"; the large boys "rasseled," at arms-length, side holts and backs, and lifted at stiff heels. At a later day when school kept in autumn or in winter, they snowballed, slid down hill or skated on the glare ice.*

Frequently, there were the singing lessons, conducted by some master of the arts and usually held in the evening in a schoolhouse centrally located. These singing schools were largely attended by the young men and women of the entire town, and to escort the young ladies to and from the singing school was not the least of its attractions for the young men. One system of singing in vogue at the time was invented by the local minister. Much of the singing was done by rote.

The town's Protestant reverend John Evans remarked: "[The] singing sounds like five hundred tunes roared out at the same time. The singers often are two-words apart, producing noises so hideous and disorderly as is bad beyond expression. The notes are prolonged so that I myself have twice in one not paused to take a breath."

Class Management

The most prominent evils that teachers constantly struggled with were tardiness and whispering during class. These were preached about and remonstrated against, but as time went on, these problems were reduced to a minimum. The attendance was reasonably regular. Most of the students lived quite close in the neighborhood, within three or four miles. An occurrence that was quite common was that, upon arrival to school, their ears, noses or faces would appear frozen from their two mile tramp to school up and down the long hills in the harsh northwest winds.

In the face of these challenges, many teacher did well and some quite poorly. There is no possible way to generalize about the success of teachers in the rural schools of the early Republic. Memorization was students' primary task. Children studied at their desks to prepare to be drilled in rote recitation by the schoolmaster.

According to the Sandwich Historical Society, the first school report, printed in 1852, stated:

It is a lengthy report and crudité for the most part, but its criticisms of policies are practical and strong. Wages paid are not stated, but in the next year's report the average for men was $12.50 per month; for women it was less than $5.00. Such disparities may have explained some underlying problems detected by the three men in their sharply worded report

We have had some competent, excellent teachers, but not enough to supply the demand…There are difficulties in securing such a class of teachers as we need…These obstacles can be removed by us. Several circumstances conspire to detract from the esteem and high repute in which the instructors of our youth should ever be held. Few public functionaries hold a more important position in society, and very few are exercising a greater influence. Low wages is one difficulty. Almost any other business is more lucrative. The meager stipend of the teacher serves to degrade the office of his own view and that of others…
In many districts the seat of their operations, their place of daily toil, would have been mistaken in the dark ages, by the casual observer, for a rendezvous of wizards or gypsies, rather than a place where an industrious and intelligent and enterprising people sent their rosy-cheeked children, to be educated for those high and responsible stations they may soon occupy.

When the teacher enters some of these filthy, ill constructed rooms and surveys the furniture, the old broken (teacher's) chair, the seat and desks hacked, scored and scratched by several generations of unlucky boys, he feels himself deeply degraded. The class of little strangers before him have come out from the tidy cottages of the neighborhood where neatness and order reign; but here disorder and turbulence is inspired by their circumstances…
Here, day after day the teacher is doomed to go the rounds of his thankless task; and for board and lodging, in many cases, to wander over the district like a common mendicant. Here are two reasons why we have not got more good teachers.

Ours is the first town in the country in respect to population and wealth; but we appropriate less money per scholar than any other town save one. Of the 211 towns in this State reporting last year, 196 appropriated from $1.01 to $5.08 per scholar, averaging more than $2.00, while this town appropriates only 93 cents to a scholar. Of the 14 towns of lower rank,

6. There will be no whispering or other disturbances. Students may only speak with the teacher's permission.

7. If any student over the age of ten, refused to obey the teacher, the student shall be expelled, and can only return with the permission of the inspectors.

8. Each student shall have his own book for reading class.

9. Each student shall be furnished with a suitable writing book, ink-stand, and ink, pen or quill, and ruler, before he is instructed in writing.

10. If any student breaks any glass or damages the school house, unless the damage is repaired in three days, he will be deprived of the privileges of the school until the damage is repaired.

11. Each scholar shall leave the school house as soon as convenient after school and go directly home unless directed otherwise.

12. It shall be the duty of the scholar to keep their books, clothes and persons neat and clean.

The school committees encouraged parents to visit their local neighborhood schools to show support for the teachers and make them less likely to become disheartened. At the time, there appeared to be much apathy in the general education occurring at the school, and it was only considered an auxiliary to assist the parent in the training of their children.

The role of the district school was clear. In a manual of the 1830s, Orville Taylor declared that "it is our duty to make men moral."

The young scholars could quickly recognize a good teacher from his or her good sense, relationship to the students and ability to win the respect, behavior and interest of the pupils. But the teachers had to deserve success before winning it, for the students met them on ground of their own choosing and made their paths smooth or difficult according to the attitude of the teachers toward them.

Frederick Packard (1794–1867), who was the author of *The Taught*, is an example of an attempt to make the path of school teachers straight and plain in his following statement: "Ever since the world began, the depraved passion of men have required some kind of restraint. Because we are the freest country in all the earth, we are more exposed than any other country to have our liberty used as a cloak for licentiousness."

Jonathan Smith, author of "Recollection of a District School," reflected on the following:

The real worth of any educational system was determined by the quality of the men and women it graduated, and what they would for themselves and

The Baker River School near the intersection of old Route 25 and the Smith Bridge Road, West Plymouth, New Hampshire. *Courtesy of the Plymouth Historical Society.*

The Crockett Schoolhouse at Laconia Bridge. The last year the school was used as such was 1922–23. Seen on the front steps is Robert W. Farnam. *Courtesy of the Meredith Historical Society.*

their country in after life. Its graduates had shown themselves equal to all calls made upon their patriotism, their courage, and enterprise, their spirit of loyalty and obedience, and intelligence and progressive sprit demanded by the mighty events which have transpired since 1861.

THE RULES OF DISCIPLINE

New Hampshire district schools were closely tied to their communities, inexpensive and under very tight control. The schoolmaster ruled his class by virtue, moral character and his governing position as headmaster of the class with the rod in hand. It is said that they taught morals, but the moral education of children in the district school was the mission of the state and not a matter of public debate. In 1840, this situation was highly discussed; school officials defended corporal punishment against parental challenges as a necessity to shape the scholars into industrious, temperate and reverent adults. Local school committees ritualistically announced that good discipline made good government, and good government in the schoolroom was a prerequisite of learning.

During the first morning of school, the master would read a very long list of rules, which were to be observed both in class and out. These regulations of behavior were strictly laid down, and God help the youth who thoughtlessly or recklessly disobeyed them. The ways of punishment were exceedingly varied and ingenious; even the ordinary black leather strap had its variations, as will be illustrated later. Much of the school time was consumed, not to say wasted, in violent exercise, participated in both by the teacher and pupil. Among the milder forms of punishment was "sitting on nothing" or "on the top end of an old-fashioned elm bark seat chair, turned down." Or the pupil would be compelled to hold out a heavy book horizontally. Stooping down to hold a nail or peg in the floor, "with an occasional smart rap on the rear" to keep the youth from bending his knees; standing in the corner; and sitting with the girls were very mild forms of punishment.

In many cases, if a boy was caught misbehaving, he was promptly called onto the floor. It was usually not long before two other boys were ready to keep number one company. The requisite number now having been obtained, the punishment "circus" began. The first offender was made to get down on his hands and knees, number two must mount on his back and the third boy was compelled to whip them soundly around the room.

This punishment was considered perfectly fair, since the boys were obliged to swap places until each had taken his turn at "whipping once and being whipped twice."

The experience was not all fun for the teachers in those one-room schools. Often the larger boys would combine forces, boldly advance on the master and, if successful in their onslaught, carry him out of the schoolhouse and boldly pitch him into the snowdrift or dunk him in some nearby brook. It required a man with some nerve to take a school where his predecessors had been severally overtaken with force and in turn ejected in this manner. On one occasion, a teacher was seen coming to school and had started the morning services, when the pupils began striding back and forth through the schoolroom; turning suddenly, the master was stern while he told the boys that if they didn't behave, he would follow them home and lick their parents.

On another occasion, a master, Mr. Adams, who taught in the Sugar Hill District in Weare, New Hampshire, had in his school as many as twenty strapping boys, each one of whom was over six feet tall. One day, at a preconceived signal, they all arose and marched in single file around the room. As the foremost boy passed the fireplace, he signaled a burning branch from the hearth and shouted to his followers, "Shoulder firelock!" However, at that point the schoolmaster took a hand in the affair and ordered, "Ground firelock! Consarnye." At the same instant, he gave the leader a blow that stretched him at full length on the floor. It is said that no better ordered school was ever taught in that district than the one taught by Master Adam that year.

Some of the punishments seemed needlessly cruel and unnecessary, but it must be remembered that corporal punishment was part of the spirit of the times. The parents knew that they had received thrashings when they went to school, and it seemed to them a necessary though painful part of the child's education.

In *History of New Hampshire*, Hobart Pillsbury records the following wisdom of punishment:

> *A certain gentleman known as,   Master Thurston, who taught for many years in Boscawen, was a noted disciplinarian, and when in those days a master was noted for "discipline" you may be sure that he deserved it. It is related that Master Thurston had as one of his instruments a black leather strap, made into two pieces with sheet lead stitched between them. On one end of this strap he had punched four holes and on the other five. His mode of procedure was this: Holding the strap in full view of the*

trembling youngster, he would ask, "Which will you have, four holes or five?" If the boy said four the master would reply, "For fear of making a mistake I will give you both." It was a current remark in West Salisbury, where Thurston taught for several years, "that the surrounding farms would not have been cleared of birch if Master Thurston had not been employed so long as a teacher."

Franklin McDuffee, in his *History of Rochester, New Hampshire*, wrote the following of a one-armed schoolmaster, a veteran of the Revolution who was a noted wielder of the birch and rod; the strength of his lost arm seemed to supplement the muscle of the one remaining. His name, Tanner, was most appropriate; the boys, indeed, deemed it the most fitting thing about him. His successor, Master Orne, was said to have been remarkable, in fact unique, in the way in which he dealt out punishment:

He flogged singly, and by classes, and by the whole school; just as officers review their soldiers, by squads, by companies, by battalions, and by regiments. It was of no use for the boy to rebel, they obtained little sympathy at home. The parents considered that it was what they had received when they went to school, and what was good enough for them was good enough for the children. It is strange how history repeats itself, even in educational matters.

There is preserved by Hobart Pillsbury the writings of Jacob N. Knapp, who taught school more than 150 years ago, an accurate picture of the school life of that time. The account runs as follows:

In the winter of my 17th year, I received an invitation to teach school for three months in Loudon, near Concord. A schoolmaster's wages were at that time $6 a month and board. My school consisted of about 40 pupils. It was composed of both sexes and all ages. Most of the children under 10 years of age wore leather aprons, reaching from their chins to their ankles. These aprons, after being worn a little time, became striped and shinning with bean porridge, which in winter made the principal food of the children. Many of the little girls took snuff; it was the fashion.

In my school I had often used signals instead of words. The exercises in reading and spelling for the day were about to commence. I, as usual, gave with the ferule on tap upon the table. The first class came out from their desks on to the open floor, and stood in line. On receiving a slight sign, the head pupil read, and then the next, and so on to the last. At receiving a blow from their teacher, each one bowed and returned noiselessly to his or her desk. Two raps upon the table called up to the second class, who were exercised and dismissed in the same manner. Three raps called up the third class. This division closed the exercises. The school was dismissed.

The people then and there considered it a privilege to board the schoolmaster. To accommodate them, I boarded in 13 different families, and thus became intimately acquainted with every individual in the district. The price of board was 4 shillings and 6 pence a week. Lived well; fat beef and pork, lambs and poultry, in their seasons; butter, honey and drop cake abounded; coffee, tea and cream were liberally supplied.

4

Master Dudley Leavitt

Master Dudley Leavitt was considered the most remarkable man for his time, being well versed in most phases in academia: mathematics, astronomy, theories of navigation and many ancient and modern languages. Dudley was born in Exeter, New Hampshire, on May 23, 1772, one of the fifty descendants from deacon John Leavitt of Hingham, Massachusetts, after coming from England in 1626.

He was the elder son of Joshua Leavitt and Elizabeth James and was named Dudley due to the fact that both his parents were descendants of Governor Thomas Dudley of the Bay Colony.

Master Leavitt was a fine scholar by the time he was twenty. He spent most of his time, hour after hour and any spare moments, in study.

Like many early pioneers, he moved north from Exeter to Gilmanton while a teenager. In 1794, he married a local girl, Judith Glidden, and at the age of twenty-two, took permanent resident in the town.

During his early twenties, he was well advanced in the sciences and mathematics. He spent much time studying Greek and Latin under his mentor, the Reverend Isaac Smith of Gilmanton. Later, he went on to study and master Hebrew, music, astronomy and navigation. Needless to say, Dudley was regarded as one of the finest minds of his day and surely the best New Hampshire had produced.

In 1806, he moved to a small farm in Meredith, located on the Range Road leading from Meredith Village to Center Harbor, where he lived to the end of his days. Just a short distance to the east on his farm lies

Portrait of Master Dudley Leavitt painted two years before his death by artist Walter Ingalls of Gilmanton, New Hampshire (oil on canvas, thirty by twenty-five inches, 1849). The portrait is presently on display at the New Hampshire Historical Society in Concord, New Hampshire, as a gift of the Committee of Nine from 1875. *Courtesy of the Meredith, Historical Society.*

SEAL OF THE STATE OF NEW HAMPSHIRE
* 1776 *

DUDLEY LEAVITT
1772-1851

Author and publisher of almanacs first appearing in 1797. Best known was "Leavitt's Farmers' Almanac and Miscellaneous Year Book" which was continued after his death for about 45 years. This publication provided information vital to domestic and agricultural life of the period. He lived in house 200 yards east.

State of New Hampshire historic plaque located on Route 25 at the town lines of Meredith and Center Harbor, New Hampshire, 1987. *Courtesy of the author.*

the Northern central bay of Lake Winnipesaukee. Beyond this point of the lake rises the Ossipee Mountain Range. To the north is Red Hill, and to the south and west ascend tablelands particularly clothed with forest and the Belknap Mountain Range. The scenic attractions of the immediate locality are marked and consist of a quiet New Hampshire homestead. Beside a country road, but little used, are large shade trees and ample farmyard verdant with closely cropped grass. His farmland was considerable, bordering Lake Winnipesaukee and the Middle Bay to Center Harbor. He cultivated his land, and made due from his crops for his large family of eleven children.

During much of his long and busy life, Master Leavitt, as he was most affectionately referred to, pursued the combined occupation of a farm, a schoolmaster, and an almanac-maker. In 1811, he completed a teacher's assistance text entitled *The Scholar's Review and Teacher's Daily Assistant*, which was "a compendium of literary and scientific works. This text was designed as a summary retrospect of the principle and most curious rules of practical knowledge; to be used by the teacher in instructing and examining his scholars; to accomplish the student in his classical and polite learning to persons of every class."

In hopes that this manuscript would be used in the classroom as an aid for teachers, Master Leavitt sent this work to A. Lyman and Company in Portland, Maine, where it was accepted, published and distributed through the East Coast as a "must" for the teacher of the common school. (This book was published while Maine was still the District of Maine, the *Scholar's Review and Teacher's Daily Assistant* was the second mathematics book to be published in the district. The first hardcover book to be published there had been printed only fourteen years earlier.) The following declaration is presented:

> *(LS.) BE IT REMEMBERED, That on the thirteenth day of August, A.D. 1811, and in the thirty-sixth year of Independence of the United States of America, A. Lyman & Co. of said District, have deposited in this office the title of a book, the right whereof they claim as proprietor, in the words following, viz.*
>
>   *In an act of congress of the United States, entitled, "An act for the encouragement of learning, by securing the copies of maps, charts, and books to the authors of proprietors of such copies, during the time therein mentioned," and also, "An act entitled, 'An act supplementary to an act,' entitled, 'An act for the encouragement of learning, by securing the*

copies of maps, charts and books, to the author of proprietors of such copies, during the times therein mentioned, and extending the benefits thereof to the arts of designing, engraving and etching historical and other prints.'"

Henry Sewall, Clerk
District Court, Maine
A True copy of record.

Master Leavitt signified in his *Scholar's Review and Teacher's Assistant* that it was important to look over or examine work more than once. He explains that without practice, even the most retentive memory would forget learned rules and facts. Students stayed bright by reviewing the subjects. When a student reviewed his studies and reduced the theory to practice, he always found things not commonly taught in school. The object of these essays was to supply what was wanted and explain what was obscure in the author's use. In reviewing the subjects, it was endeavored to converge the sense of focus or condense it into as few words as possible so that the reader could comprehend them at a single glance.

It had been found that nothing was more conducive to improving learners' knowledge than when the teacher would examine them often. This method had often been neglected for want of books to assist them. The trouble of tumbling over the library of authors, encumbered with notes and prolix examples, had an effect to introduce into schools confusion, where everything ought to be clear and regular.

A considerable part of the summary of the manuscript supposed the reader to have studied the rules it contained. The purpose was to light the candle of knowledge.

Let us examine the first page of this school exercise. Master Leavitt entitles it "Language" with his definition as follows:

The word language signifies vocal sounds, or sounds from the mouth. The term is derived from the Latin word, Lingua, *a tongue; whence language is sometimes called a tongue, because the tongue is the instrument of speech. It is proper to say we understand a person's language when he conveys his ideas by signs, for the word is from the Latin* Signum, *which signifies a mark or token.*

Compare this to Weld's *Parsing Book*'s rules of grammar:

Language
Rules for Grammatical Composition

In all literary composition there are five principal things to be considered.
1. The text, or subject to be treated of.
2. Grammar, or the rules of agreement, government, orthography, and punctuation.
3. Reason, or Logic, whose office is to convince by undeniable argument.
4. Elegance, or Rhetoric, whose office is to arrange, persuade, please, and move the passions.
5. Style, or the mode of expression best suited to the subject.

There are three kinds of style, used in speaking and writing, viz. The simple, middle, and sublime. The simple style is used to teach; the middle to delight; and the sublime, to move. Again, the simple, or low style, is fit for comedy, or plays representing the most common and familiar actions. The middle, for history; and the sublime, for tragedy, of the lofty sort of plays in which great personages are brought on the stage, and the subject is also suitable for common conversation.

Style is also distinguished by the terms concise and diffuse. The concise style is that in which the ideas are expressed in a few words. The diffuse is that in which the same ideas are repeated over and over, or connected by flowing phraseology, in relation of foreign or trifling circumstances.

Note: Such style, says Cicero, should always be used, as will express great things magnificently: middle things moderately; and low things simply.

Poetry

According to Dudley Leavitt: "A verse in poetry is so called from the Latin verso, to turn, because when one line is completed we turn back to another. Each line of verse consists of a number of feet, and each foot of a number of syllables. When a single syllable is taken by itself, it is called a 'cesura.' In polysyllables, the last syllable but one is called penult, and the last but two the antepenult. A long syllable requires double the time to pronounce it that a short one does." He continues to detail the rules of poetry:

Practical Rules
English poetry, has only four kinds of measure, viz.
    1. Iambic, which comprises verses of four, six, eight, or ten syllables.
    2. Trochaic, which comprises lines of three, five, or seven syllables
    3. Dactyl, which begins with a short syllable and ends with a long one,
and contains three Dactyls in a line, exclusive of the five and last syllables.
    4. Anapaestic, which consists of two short, and one long syllable, every
third being accented.

Note: It is a general rule in writing poetry that the last syllable of the second foot should be accented—This rule excludes Dactyl verse.

Note: In reading verse, the caesural pause, or pause of one syllable, answers to a comma in prose, and is most graceful after the 4th, 5th, 6th, or 7th syllables. The final pause, must be observed at the end of every line, whether there be a stop or not; but when there is no stop written or understood, at the close of a line, the voice must only be suspended the length of the caesural pause, but not elevated or depressed.

Note: Scanning, is determining the number of feet on any line, and what kind they are.

MUSIC AS TAUGHT IN THE RURAL SCHOOLS OF NEW HAMPSHIRE

These instructions were written in *The Scholar's Review and Teacher's Daily Assistant.* They are as follows:

Music is one of the seven liberal sciences belonging to the Mathematical and considers the number, time and tune of sounds.

Vocal Music
Practical rules and directions for a chorister and company of singers are to be observed in performing sacred music in public worship.
    1. It would be conducive to the improvement, as well as to the propriety of the performance of music, if the person who takes the lead would furnish every singer with a list of such tunes as are suitable, and intended to be

practiced, in the various meters and keys, and to assist and encourage the performers by every laudable method, to practice those tunes frequently, in different words, and endeavor to perform themselves in the nature and spirit of music.

2. When a psalm or hymn is named to be sung, the singers should observe every word with the greatest attention so as to know what words ought to be performed loud, soft, lively, grave, &c.

3. As soon as the subject is read, let the chorister distinctly name the tune; then give each part its true pitch, in a full distinct, yet soft sound: the performers in every part should sound the pitch with the chorister, in the same manner. Then observing the most accurate and uniform time, let the whole performance be with dignity, solemnity, and in the most moving and animating manner which the united powers of good language, proper gestures, timely graces, and harmonious sounds are able to inspire.

DUDLEY LEAVITT THE AUTHOR, HISTORIAN AND MASTER SCHOLAR

Here in the small village of Meredith, Leavitt continued to prepare and edit school textbook for publishers throughout New England. Many were widely used throughout the Northeast as well as Europe. Year after year, he made the calculations whose results were embodied in the calendars of his famous *Almanack*. From 1811 to 1817, and perhaps longer, he compiled the annual issues of the *New Hampshire Register* and was the first to enrich its pages with brief records of memorable events.

For a time, he also prepared the calendar for the *Freewill Baptist Register*. Some of his other books included: The *Elements of Arithmetick Made Easy*, published in Exeter, the complete *Directory for parsing the English Language*, and *Juvenile Geography*, published at the state capital in 1829. He wrote many books and pamphlets on drawing, music and many other sciences, of which his mind was a complete storehouse. He was constantly in pursuit of knowledge and often, when at work on his farm, would stop, go into his home, look up some point in reference and then go back to his work and meditation.

In his 1830 text, *The Teacher Assistant and Scholars Mathematical Directory*, Dudley Leavitt gives the follow preface:

Every instructor of schools knows that in almost every school, many different arithmetics are used; each containing more or less questions of a curious nature of rather different solutions. These questions, the ingenious and inquisitive student, is anxious to solve, and after puzzling awhile, applies to the instructor for assistance, who perhaps solves them, but their investigation and solution frequently requires more time than can well be spared in a school where many different branches of education are taught. Sometimes questions are found in a book which contains no rules or precedent for solving them. The consideration of these circumstances induced the author to compose this little manual by the help of which most of the difficult questions are found in any mathematical treatise commonly used in schools may be solved or explained.

March 20, 1830
Dudley Leavitt

Master Leavitt maintained that mathematics and other disciplines should be mastered by the teacher and students who had not learned to distinguish between plain questions and riddles. If the teacher did not immediately attend to and solve every question, the pupil would conclude that the master could not do his duty as a teacher properly. Therefore, the teacher had to follow the proper key of grammar.

Upon examining Master Leavitt's *Directory for Parsing the English Language being a new Grammatical Essay*, Leavitt's educational philosophy becomes more pronounced as a supplement to Lindley Murray's grammar commonly used in schools and as a recapitulation of the practical principles and rules.

"My young reader: It must be pleasing to you and to your parents for you to learn what form or shape the world is of, how large it is, what part of it is land and what part is water," Leavitt wrote in his touching "Author's Address to the Student," in his *Juvenile Geography*. In his works, he promises to tell them the location of all the important places mentioned in the Bible and then to tell them about Columbus's discovery of America, where Captain Cook was killed, where Robinson Crusoe was supposed to have lived and

what countries produced the imitative Ape, the Majestick Lion, the huge Elephant, the growling tiger and leopard, and the whining crocodile. All these things, and many more, you may learn by studying this little book, and the knowledge you thus acquire, will be an advantage to you while studying larger books on the same subject, when you are old enough to read them.

NO. LXV.

LEAVITT'S
FARMER'S
ALMANACK,
AND MISCELLANEOUS YEAR BOOK,
FOR THE YEAR OF OUR LORD
1861:

BEING THE FIRST AFTER BISSEXTILE, OR LEAP YEAR, AND, UNTIL
JULY FOURTH, THE EIGHTY-FIFTH OF AMERICAN INDEPENDENCE.

CALCULATIONS, AS TO THE LATITUDE AND LONGITUDE, SO ░░ TO
ANSWER FOR ALL THE NEW ENGLAND STATE░░░░░

Containing, with ░░e more than useful Astronomical Calcula░░░░░ a larger qu░░-
tity ░░d gre░░er variety than are to be found in ann░░░░░ Almanack of

░░░░░R, USEFUL, CURIOUS, A░░ ENTERTAINING.

PUBLICATION COMMENCED░░░░░,

BY DUDLEY ░AVITT,
TEACHER OF MATHEMATICS AND ASTRONOMY.

CALCULATIONS ACCORDING TO TRUE SOLAR TIME.

Year after year rolls on. The Sun, and Moon,
And Stars, and all the Planets, speak the praise
Of Him, their great Creator, who first called
Them into being, by his almighty power.

CONCORD:
EDSON C. EASTMAN.

Entered, according to Act of Congress, in the year 1860, by JOHN F. BROWN, in the
Clerk's Office of the District Court of the District of New Hampshire.

Cover of *Leavitt's Farmer's Almanack, and Agricultural Register* (1861). *Courtesy of
the author.*

In spite of all the wonderful achievements, Master Leavitt was chiefly known for his *Almanack*. Its first number was published in January 1797, when George Washington was president of the United States and the country itself was but eight years old. It spans much of the time of the Republic's existence, having lived through all the successive periods of the war of 1812 and the Civil War. Dudley Leavitt's *Almanack* was considered the second-longest published work of any American almanac (the *Old Farmer's Almanac* being the longest).

Leavitt's *Almanack* was issued under various titles (and spellings) and has lasted for over 144 years. Master Leavitt edited his almanac ever year until his death in 1851. Here he supplied all matters and made all weather conditions and astronomical calculations. "I have endeavored to make the calculations of my *Almanack* accurate," Leavitt wrote in the 1797 edition, "but as the printers gave me but short notice, the time allowed to prepare my calendar for the press, may perhaps have occasioned some trifling errors."

The Honorable Joseph A. Walker of the general court of New Hampshire wrote of Mr. Leavitt and his *Almanack*:

> *It rarely happens that a small manual, annually issued for temporary use, completes in undiminished vigor of life of one hundred years. This, however, Mr. Dudley Leavitt's* Almanac *[sic] has done with fair prospect of living thru another century, 1896.*

The master always took the scientific attitude of the astronomer over the prophetic attitude of the astrologer, perhaps accounting for surviving testimonials about the "Little Book's" (as the *Almanack* was referred to) value and worth.

"The sight of the almanac hanging on the nail in the kitchen has been familiar to thousands of son and daughters during the 1800's when it was considered the bible of farming," Leavitt's nephew and student, William B. Leavitt, wrote in the 1912 edition. It was Dudley's nephew, William, who continued the yearly almanac, writing and publishing into the twentieth century.

The holes punched not too neatly through the upper left-hand corner of the almanac, preserved in the New Hampshire Historical Society's collection, seem to support this romantic image. Even though no concentrated effort was apparently made to distribute and promote this almanac, the 1846 edition had a circulation of over sixty thousand copies and went through two printings.

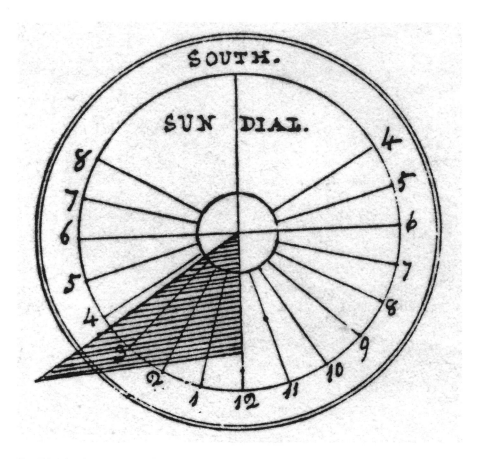

Sun Dial for Astronomical Calculations. *Courtesy of the Meredith Historical Society and* Leavitt's Farmer's Almanack.

Enclosed is a letter dated June 1841 to Leavitt's publisher regarding some changes and additions to upcoming almanacs:

Mr. Brown, Sir,

If you will hand or forward the enclosed letters, as directed, as soon as convenient, you will confer a favour.

If you can procure Gregory's Mathematicks for Practical Men, and send it to me by the stage, I will allow you the cast for it, out of the next payment towards the Almanack.

If you put a new Cent to the title page of the Almanack, I think a Sun dial, such as here enclosed would be the most appropriate for such a work.

> *There will probably be a new arrangement of Courts in this State, at the June Session of the Legislature. Let nothing prevent an accurate list being inserted in the almanac for 1842. If necessary send me the proof sheets of the Courts and I will read and return it.*
> *Yours, respectfully,*
> *Dudley Leavitt.*

Enclosed is a very sensitive letter, in his handwriting, requesting a teaching position in the local common school in Meredith, New Hampshire, so as to compensate his income for the support of his family and farm during his early days in the township. It reads as follows:

> *Meredith, April. 17th. 1811*
>
> *Dear Sir.*
> *I should like to take a school for the term of one quarter to commence to the middle of May next. If you hear of any vacancy in your neighborhood, for a teacher duly recommended, and will confer another particular favor on your obedient friend and humble servant.*
> *Dudley Leavitt.*

Thirteen years after Dudley moved to Meredith (August 1819), he opened his Meredith Academic School. There he taught at least one term each year until he was seventy-four years old. In an advertisement, published in the *Concord Observer*, he announced:

> *No pains will be spared to render the acquisition of useful knowledge, easy and pleasant to the young ladies and gentlemen who may attend the school. Reasonable tuition was $3.00 per quarter. Except for teaching algebra, navigation, gunnery, or the science of projectile, geometry, trigonometry, astronomy, and philosophy for which the tuition will be $3.50 per quarter and in proportion for any length of time. Dudley Leavitt hereby respectfully, gives this information that he proposes to open his school at his home in Meredith near Centre Harbor, on the 23rd day of August next.*

For nearly half a century, Mr. Leavitt lived on his farm in Meredith, which produced little and only partially supported his family. It was here that he received his pupils and taught them the common branches of learning. When the master was not with his own academic school,

Meredith, Apr. 17th 1811.

Dear Sir:

I should like to take a School for the term of one quarter, to commence the middle of May next. If you hear of any vacancy in your neighborhood, for a teacher duly recommended, and will inform me by letter via Centre-Harbor Post-Office, you will confer another particular favor on your obedient friend and humble servant,

Dudley Leavitt.

Geo. Frost, Esqr.

C.S. — Would thank you, Sir, to state the wages.

D.L.

Letter of request from Dudley Leavitt for a teaching position, Meredith, April 17, 1811. *Courtesy of the author.*

he would travel to many of the surrounding communities and provide instruction in their common district schools, but he concentrated his teaching to schoolhouse Number Four in Meredith on the stage route to Center Harbor. This house is no longer in existence; however, it is believed to have been located a quarter of a mile from the Quarry Road on Route 25.

Master Leavitt was known for his scrupulous politeness, love of knowledge and reverence for the elderly. To say the least, he was strict in the classroom, as was then considered necessary, but his knowledge and ability was so greatly admired by his pupils, who came long distances to learn of him, that they gave their utmost attention to his teaching.

DUDLEY LEAVITT, THE FAMILY MAN

In civic affairs, there is very little evidence of Master Leavitt's involvement in community activities; however, the Gilman Town record of the annual meeting held on March 11, 1802, indicates that Dudley Leavitt was chosen one of the selectmen, and at the adjoined meeting on March 18, he was, at his request, excused and Thomas Bogswell Esq. chosen to replace him.

On March 13, 1804, Dudley Leavitt was chosen to be town clerk. The following year on March 12, he was reelected, and on March 14, 1806, he was chosen a third time to this post; however, on the August 26 of that same year, he resigned, and Dr. Simon Foster was chosen to the office. It was at this time that Mr. Leavitt moved to the village of Meredith. Dudley Leavitt was considered to be a God-fearing man with devout respect for the scriptures, according to the Meredith Historical Society's 1976 biography. His wife, Judith, was a member of the local Congregational Church. Dudley was not a member but attended services regularly with Judith. One evening, Judith stood up in church and fervently prayed for her husband's salvation. After her public plea on her husband's behalf, Dudley stood and responded, "We read in God's word: That the unbelieving husband shall be justified by the prayers of his believing wife." Then he picked up his hat and walked out.

He was the father of eleven children, nine of whom lived to adulthood. They were all scholars in their own right. One of his sons, Dudley Junior, prepared for the ministry after graduating from Dartmouth College, but he died suddenly only a few hours before his classmates received their licenses at the Andover Theological Seminary in Andover, Massachusetts.

Master Leavitt was "active in his motions and full of kindness to all. Tall and spare in form; abstemious in his habits, and filling up with usefulness, and left not a single enemy behind him," wrote the almanac publisher Mr. Brown. One of his former students described him as "very polite; even to his small children he would tip his hat and bow." Townspeople remembered seeing him when he was working on his Meredith farm. He would stop

Home of Dudley Leavitt in Meredith, New Hampshire. *Photo courtesy by E.W. Smith of Centre Harbor.*

whatever he was doing to answer a question, give assistance to a neighbor or satisfy his own curiosity. It almost seemed that a life so protracted, so busy, so regular, so quiet and so widely useful as his was might flow on indefinitely.

To universal regret, on Monday, the September 15, 1851, his active hands and mind ceased to guide him. He fell dead at the place he loved best: his home. He must have known of the oncoming event, for just a few months earlier, he had transferred most of his property to his eldest son, Isaac.

This farm was considered one of the finest in town. It had a wealth of pine trees and many valuable acres on the shore of Lake Winnipesaukee. The shore property was eventually left to the Town of Meredith as a public park.

5

Reflections of Yesterday's One-Room Schools

*On the highway corner the schoolhouse stands
Under an elm tree broad and tall;
And rollicking children in laughing bands,
Come at the master's warning call.*

The following are reflections of the one-room schools in New Hampshire. These stories are based on fact; however, they contain embellishment by the author.

The country district school has been the subject of much discussion and censure, according to the point of view taken by the critics who have essayed and passed judgment on its merits and demerits as an educational force. It must not, however, be compared with our present standards of the twenty-first century To estimate it justly, it should be considered in the light of the social and industrial conditions of a century ago, and the demands made by those conditions upon its scholars when grown to manhood and womanhood. The results of its training on its pupils, too, are important factors in the scholars' forming a correct opinion of its worth or worthlessness as an instrument of moral and intellectual culture.

The social and industrial lives of the people of the district need to be carefully considered if a correct opinion is to be formed. Most of the residents were farmers, their farms varying from fifty to two hundred acres each. Each farmer cultivated his property himself with the assistance of their sons, while the mothers, with the assistance of their daughters, attended to the work

Quimby School House No. 11, North Sandwich. During the mid-1800s, there were as many as twenty-five district schools in Sandwich. These one-room schools were considered neighborhood schools. In 1825, there were as many as 790 students attending the Sandwich district schools. The small building on the right was used as the outhouse. *Courtesy of the author.*

of the home. They employed no outside labor, unless, for a few days in the busy season, and then it was usually found in the neighborhood. I doubt there was a labor-saving machine for a farm or house in the district, and the children were trained into experts in the use of all the hand tools for farm and household use.

The parents were conservative and very independent in their ways of thinking and doing, averse to innovation, patient, plodding, law-abiding and happy if, at the end of the year, their income had equaled their expenditures. Surplus help found ready employment on the farms and in the homes of the neighborhood, though sometimes one would seek a temporary place in one of the small mills in the village. During the winter season, all the boys and girls came together at the parental hearthstone "to go to school."

The family farms were modest but comfortable. Few could boast of more than two carpets. Not a house had a piano or parlor organ, though a few families had a melodeon or some such instrument. The people were intelligent readers and thinkers on the questions of the day's activities. Besides the local paper, little outside news was read in the home. Almost without exception the families were descendants of the early settlers of the town. From the father and mother down to the smallest six-year-old child, all worked hard, patiently and continuously. They were regular attendees at church, and no intemperance or other disorder ruffled the peace of the community.

The problem of the district school was to educate and qualify its pupils for the social and industrial situations then existing. Its supporters did not and could not foresee the vast changes that were soon to come, nor could the people have met them in their educational system if they had. The school, in its organization and general character, was the natural outgrowth of the conditions by which it was surrounded, and by these it is to be judged.

There were few schoolhouses in those days, and most of them were one-room buildings set apart on land not very desirable as a place for the school. There are few memories to recall the schools of yesterday that may be more dear or most lasting to us who remember houses of learning. The incidents and events of the intervening period have fled like a forgotten dream, but the associations of our school life have become fixed on our minds. Our parents delighted whenever they found the opportunity, to describe their own school days in North Sandwich. How grandmother's eyes would kindle as she spoke of those good old days when the boys wore cocked hats, buckskin breeches and long stockings reaching to the knees and tied with garters ornamented with silver buckles. The master wore a wig more than one hundred years ago or had his hair braided and hanging down his back.

The pupils had no desks in this very primitive school building for learning, and often their seats were simple slabs of wood laid on rude blocks of logs sawed, it may have been, from the huge backlog at that time burning on the blazing hearth. More often than not, two or three books would have to meet the needs of a large class—or maybe the parents loaned them a Bible to read—and these books were passed along from one to another as the turn came to read.

Some crack in the floor was usually selected as the boundary line for the class, and along the arbitrary mark each one of the pupils was expected to place his or her toe, and woe to the one who happened to miss it by a fraction of an inch. At the stern command of the master, "Tension!" everyone ducked his head, and immediately the one at the head began to read, passing the book to the next as soon as he had reached the end of a paragraph. At the close of the reading exercise, the master would put them through a severe course of spelling, and whoever missed a word had to drop to the end of the line, while the fortunate speller took his place with an air of triumph. It was thought a great disgrace to be at the foot of the class, and some of the hardest mental fights were fought in the spelling class.

There were really only three major studies during that time—the three Rs: "reading, 'riting and 'rithmetic." The writing paper was very scarce and more expensive than books. The ink was made by boiling the bark of the white maple, and pens were made from goose quills. It was considered an honor to be able to sharpen these pens properly, and the boy who was selected by the master to do this as the day's hour in the practice of penmanship began was looked upon with envy by the other pupils. The inkstand was made from the tip of some ox horn sawed off at the right length, and a wooden plug fitted into the bottom with a smaller one at the top.

Naturally the discipline was most severe. The master held the undisputed right to punish his pupils according to his will, and it was generally understood that the boy who was flogged at school should receive a duplicate chastisement at home.

Thus, the majority of the masters whacked even the big boys over the head at their pleasure, and the master blistered his hand with the heavy white birch ferule that he carried with him even more closely than our policemen do a side arm.

It is possible the boy had this contingency in mind when he was asked how he liked to go to school and replied that he liked the going well enough, and the coming was all right; being there was what he didn't like.

With all the rigid discipline, it frequently happened that the boys sometime got the upper hand of the master. I have heard said where the master had resolved to give up teaching and go to chopping wood when he received a note from an unknown source requesting him to give the school another day of teaching. Accordingly, though not without some misgivings, he opened the school the following morning. All the big "mischief-making" pupils were present, and he knew from the general appearance that a crisis was about to take place. He had barely finished the morning exercise, when a horseman rode up to the front door, dismounted and marched into the room without the formality of knocking. He was a tall, large man dressed in a fur coat, which made him look much larger, and he carried in his hand a heavy, green-hide whip. Glancing sharply over the surprised assembly, he said in a clear, penetrating voice:

"With your master's permission, I wish to teach you a short lesson in good behavior. I will make it brief but impressive."

Without further words this stranger then began to ply his large whip furiously over the heads and shoulders of those refractory young men, and so swiftly and furiously did he wage his attacks that the whole scene was over before the terrified victims could rally sufficiently to make a united

The little red one-room schoolhouse was called True and located on Chick's Corner on Holderness Road. This building remains privately owned and is in mint condition. *Courtesy of the author.*

resistance. Never was such a flogging undertaken and carried out within the knowledge of those present. When the last rebellious subject had been dealt with to his liking, while the amazed master looked on with trepidation, the stranger called the school to order, saying: "I have ridden a hundred miles, more or less, to give you that lesson, and I hope you will never forget it. Now, Master—go, on with your school, and just as sure as you need me again I shall come. And where I have given one blow this morning I will give twain next time."

Then, with an air of deep gratification, he marched slowly out of the house, mounted his horse and rode away. There may have been those who could have disclosed his identity, but if so, they died with the secret locked in their bosoms. As he never returned to the house, we are reasonably sure his lesson was well learned.

The small, one-story structures became the representative edifice for educational purposes. Most of these schools were not painted; however, some were and became known as the "Little Red Schoolhouse," and the American system of education was styled under that name. Today, as we travel some of the country roads, we will see the buildings painted red even though many are presently private homes.

At the beginning of the twentieth century, a poet by the name of Frank N. Scott wrote a poem about "The Little Red School-house":

How dear to this heart are the scenes where I wandered,
In the days when a boy I lived on the farm,
The ground where I played, and the seat where I pondered
On beauties of Nature that only could charm
The brook and the meadow, the bars that stood by it,
The walk where the lilacs were sparkling with dew;
The shady piazza, the rose that grew nigh it,
The little red school-house my infancy knew—
The little red school-house, how will I remember
The little red school-house my infancy knew.

The wide-spreading elm and the seat that stood near it,
The little hill pasture where hollyhooks grew;
The little red school-house, I can't but revere it,
With its wide open doors, and curtains of blue,
How often I went there with mind that was glowing,
To learn what was good and beautiful, true,
Where stores of rich learning were full, overflowing,
The little red school-house my infancy knew—
The little red school-house, how well I remember
The little red school-house my infancy knew.

How gentle the teacher gave each admonition;
How quickly I made them at home in my heart;
They've fitted my life in its every condition,
And hard has it been from those lessons to part.
And now when the years that are rapidly going,
Are leaving the wrinkles we all of us rue,
When thin are my locks, and the silver is showing,
I think of the school-house my infancy knew—
The little red school-house, how well I remember
The little red school-house my infancy knew.

CONCORD PUBLIC SCHOOLS: A HISTORY

The history of the public schools of Concord, New Hampshire, for the first century of its existence as a town was not unlike that of other towns. Up to 1805, there was no such organization as a school district.

According to Hamilton D. Hurd, historian and author of the 1885 *History of Merrimack & Belknap Counties, New Hampshire*, compiled from the town records the following excerpts:

> *The first school established in Concord was in 1731 and its support was assumed by the town in 1733. It was taught by a master hired by the selectmen, and for many years was kept in four different sections. Of the town viz.: East Concord, West Concord, Hopkinton road and Main Street. After 1766 winter schools were supported in each of the localities. The first school-house in Concord was built in 1742, and stood at the point near the northwest corner of the State-House park.*
>
> *As early as 1800 an unsuccessful effort was made by the town to divide the territory of Concord into school districts and to raise money for the building of school-houses in such districts. This effort was successfully renewed in 1807. The town appointed a committee of twenty, with the selectmen, to divide the town into school districts, in accordance with the law passed two years before, and that committee reported sixteen districts definitely described.*
>
> *The first committee to visit schools, appointed by the town, was in 1818, and the report of such committee was first ordered to be printed in 1827, for distribution among the inhabitants.*
>
> *In 1873–74 there were thirty-two schools in the district.*

From that time forth, the schools in the state united and complied with the laws for the administration of the public district school by the State of New Hampshire:

A Sample School Report and History of a Typical New Hampshire Town

1. I have here a report of the school committee for the year 1845, and we find them struggling for better schools. I'd like to share with you a portion of this short report, and ask you to recognize a few familiar phrases. Quote: "There are twenty-three school districts in the town. The 1st and 15th district, receive the largest sums; the former $204.11, and the later $122.23. The two districts receiving the least are the 19th and 22nd. The former receives $16.30, and the latter $8.87. There were thirty instructors employed during the year. Twenty-four were examines and received certificates."

2. Attention was called to, "a sad decline in the government of the school—as well as in the family. Some stated they were pained in their visit to some schools to witness the absence of necessary discipline—and while they did not recommend severity, then the teacher was to have order and not 'spare the rod.'"

3. In a 1855 school report, it was stated that the "evil of too great a variety of text books still exists in most schools." It notes no improvement in school houses—yet the buildings were a threat to health, and one paragraph is devoted to the fact that, "young people enter the school houses—lawfully if they can—forcibly if they must—and occupy them as places of social resort, at time in midnight carousels in violation of the Sabbath and to the disturbance of the neighbors. We recommend that efficient measures be adopted to prevent disorderly conduct."

4. When mother was a very small child she attended the Union School located at the town line, where the scholars sat in one town and the teacher sat in the other. The walk to school was about two miles by going across a large pasture belonging to Arthur Flanders. Mr. Flanders was a farmer with a large heard of cattle. And the bull which was lawfully grazing with the cows, would bellow and paw the ground as the three little girls crossed his domain twice each day. Nothing ever happened to them, but it was the Lord's protection.

Signed: Benjamin Plummer
Giles Leach
John K. Young

The following narrative, which was provided by friends and relatives of Sandwich, New Hampshire, contains real events, places and characters. This was a time when the one-room school was an active family and community affair.

LEARNIN' DAYS

How distinct the school raised to existence on Vittum Hill. This was the seat of our early learning experiences.

The old schoolhouse stood next to the stage route in East Sandwich, which ran from Moultonborough to Conway. Typical of the district

This annex entrance was very typical of most schoolhouses, where the students could hang their belongings and lunches. At the far end was a door leading to a supply closet. The schoolhouse was originally located on Moultonborough Neck; however, it was moved to its present location on Route 25 beside the historical building in the center of the town. *Photo courtesy of Norman Alkinson and the Moultonborough Historical Society.*

Students posing for their class picture at the local village school, 1901. *Courtesy of the Meredith Historical Society.*

school, the building was quite small with an outhouse directly to the rear of the building.

When entering East School Number One on Vittum Hill, the visitor would notice that it is like most typical one-room schoolhouses. It had two doors that opened to the classroom. The door on the left was for the boys, and the door on the right was for the girls. The room was extremely limited in space—just enough for the reading and spelling parade. At the opposite end of the room was the teacher's desk, raised on a five-inch platform from the floor. The fireplace, or potbelly stove, was usually on the north side of the room. The ventilation was extremely poor. The back seats were so high that the students could not enjoy the curiosity of the travelers as they passed on the coach road near the Ossipee Range. As visitors travel by the school in East Sandwich, they would notice that it remains the same today as it original appeared years ago.

FIRST DAY

The typical school experience for a local student began at the age of four. It was evident that the parents were too busy on the farm to assist in the fundamentals of reading or even learning the letters of the alphabet. Within time, the students began to read their first primer. Finally, the Perry spelling book completed students' readiness for the debut at summer school.

The new students never forgot their first day of school, for they thought it was the most important day of their lives. On that memorable day, students wore their finest going-to-church clothes and carried their lunch baskets proudly as they skipped to school for the first time.

Miss Martin was the students' first teacher, and she noticed their nervousness when they first met. She tried to comfort them while they slowly walked to their desks in their respective rows. Proudly, but reluctantly, each of the students followed Miss Martin about the room to their assigned desks; they were beginning to feel welcome and quietly relaxed at their assigned places in the classroom.

First on the agenda for the morning was the alphabet and simple reading assignments. Soon one of the students would become restless and search for some relief from this discomfort. Miss Martin spoke words of sympathy rather than speaking in a stern voice. When the student grew drowsy, he would drop into sleep. Miss Martin gently positioned him at length on his seat and let him fall into slumber.

Soon, most of the students of the first summer school session were quite successful in their studies, and most enjoyed their time with Miss Martin as a teacher. They really did not want to leave until the winter session began, for there was no pleasure in reciting the ABCs all alone.

During the time between the summer and winter sessions, each student was given assignments in his or her new parsing and spelling books.

The *Parsing Book* contained the rules of syntax and models for analyzing and transposing with selections of prose and poetry from writers of standard authority. This work was authored by Allen H. Weld, who suggested the principal object of analyzing and parsing was to examine the structure of sentences, change and modify composed words to render the lesson more interesting and useful in mental training, notice the importance of every word and substitute one word for another that would be similar in meaning. Each selection of students' work would be arranged to follow the general exercises of parsing.

MODIFICATION OF WORDS.

NOUN OR PRONOUN.

A noun or pronoun may be modified
1. By a noun in apposition; as, George, the king.
2. By an adjective; as, A tall mast.
3. By a preposition with its object (adjunct); as, A life of toil.
4. By a participle; as, The sun rising.
5. By a verb in the infinitive; as, A time to die.
6. By a relative clause; as, I, who speak with you.
7. Rarely by an adverb; as, Not my feet only.

VERB OR PARTICIPLE.

A verb or participle may be modified
1. By a noun in the objective case, if the verb is transitive; as, The sun gives light.
2. By a verb in the infinitive; as, He hopes to return.
3. By a preposition with its object; as, I walk in the grove.
4. By a clause; as, I hope that you are well.
5. By an adjective; as, The wind blows fresh.

ADJECTIVE.

An adjective may be modified
1. By an adverb; as, Very rich.
2. By a verb in the infinitive; as, Pleasant to behold.
3. By a preposition with its object; as, True to nature.
4. By another adjective; as, Deep blue; Liverpool deep blue earthen pitchers.

ADVERB.

An adverb may be modified
1. By another adverb; as, Most assuredly.
2. By a preposition with its object (adjunct); as, Agreeably to nature, most of all.

PREPOSITION.

A preposition may be modified
1. By an adverb; as, Far beyond.
2. By a noun in the objective case; as, Over the hills.

COMPOUND SENTENCES.

A Compound Sentence is made up of two or more simple sentences joined by connectives. CONNECTIVES are, 1. Conjunctions; 2. Conjunctive Adverbs; 3. Relative words See Gram. §112, or Parsing Book, pages 6, 7.

NOUNS INDEPENDENT.

Nouns which have no grammatical connection with the subject or predicate of a sentence, are said to be independent; as. O virtue!

ANALYSIS OF SENTENCES.

A Sentence may be analyzed by dividing it into the parts of which it is composed, and explaining their relations.

1. Divide the sentence into its two general parts, viz: the Subject or Modified Subject, the Predicate or Modified Predicate.

2. Explain the mutual relations, and point out the office of every word which has any modifying influence.

CLASSIFICATION OF SENTENCES.

1. Declarative; as, I write.
2. Interrogative; as, Do you write?
3. Imperative; as, Buy the truth.
4. Subjunctive; as, If it rains.
5. Exclamatory; as, How much he resembles his father!

The lesson for the "Modification of Words" taken from the *Parsing Book* by Allen H. Weld. *Courtesy of the author.*

The teacher for the summer school on the Center Harbor Road, 1870, is located in the back row, third from left. *Courtesy of the Meredith Historical Society.*

Perry's *Only Sure Guide* is presently out of use. It is nowhere to be found, except in fragments in some dark corner of a country cupboard or shelf at the local historical society. All vestiges of it will disappear forever.

After the morning studies, there was some recess time; however, it was a limited to physical activities that could be done in a small playground space. The children really didn't mind, for they had indoor activity also.

When the winter session had finally arrived, students memorized the repetitive ab, eb, ib, ob, ub, etc., for the days and weeks. As the students mastered the skills assigned to them, most of the students were soon assigned to work with the older boys. The students who really excelled might be put at the head of the spelling line.

One young student was called to the front of the class. Gradually, he was put at the head of the spelling line. When the boys had completed the spelling parade, the young student looked up among the older boys as he strutted to his seat. His only thought was that he was the best among the big boys. Now he held his book in his hand, and instead of standing like a little boy with his hands at his side, he proudly advanced to his desk.

As the term drew to a close, the students began to learn some self-selected pieces to recite for their final day's presentation. A good number of the students learned hymns, while many of the younger students wanted to present a poem that was written by Mrs. Peaslee, a visiting teacher from Moultonborough. They did not write compositions.

THE FINAL DAY FOR EXAMINATION

On the day of final examinations, the morning classes were shortened so the classroom could be properly cleaned, decorated and arranged for their parents, the Superintending Committee, Reverend Evans and other local guests who lived in the neighborhood. After the housekeeping was complete, the students occupied their time reviewing their poems for the afternoon exercises and presentation.

The teacher directed students to eat their lunch early, for the visitors would arrive soon. They should be properly prepared.

Shortly, the visitors began to arrive, and soon the room would be full. Parents, older brothers and sisters as well as the expected guests were in attendance.

Everyone present sat quietly in their chairs awaiting the beginning of the final day of examination presentations. Miss Martin presented a brief speech of appreciation to her students, parents and friends. On the display table were the writing books, cyphering manuscripts and gathered piles on the front desk. Presently, the writing books were examined. The pile was lifted from the table and scattered along through the hands of the visitors. Many parents were commended for the neatness with which they kept their writing assignments.

Then was the time for the arithmetic examination. The students' assignment in their presentation was to recite the rules required in this branch of study. Unfortunately, Ralph could not repeat more than half the rules. What shame and confusion Ralph felt when the students were questioned in arithmetic. Next came the display in grammar, that of parsing. A special piece was selected that they had to parse and on which they had to again drill so as to become as familiar with the parts of speech.

It was the little ones who were first to present their spelling words, reciting from their primers and answering questions from a catechism, questions such as:

1. What state do you live in?
2. What is the governor's name?
3. What country do you live it?
4. What is the president's name?

So the examination went on with the old classes. Meanwhile, ciphering books and written samples were passed among the parents and visitors. At the conclusion of the examination, the teacher asked the visitors if there were any questions or remarks to be made to the students. Praise was given to the pupils and teacher alike.

At the conclusion of the final day's examination, the Reverend Evans rose to his feet. All was silent as they listened to his closing remarks, which were directed to the students. "You are all fine and obedient students; however, you should mind your parents and not neglect your Parsing and Spelling books during vacation. Remember, all work and no play makes Jack a dull boy; all play and no work makes Jack a mere toy."

Opposite, top: A class picture at the Bridge School in Holderness, 1930. *Courtesy of the Holderness Historical Society.*

Opposite, bottom: The True School as it appears today on Vittum Hill in East Sandwich. Today, the old schoolhouse on Vittum is one of the finest restored buildings in the town of Sandwich. *Courtesy of the author.*

Schoolhouse in Moultonborough. Doris waits quietly at the front door for her father to take her home. *Courtesy of the Moultonborough Historical Society.*

At the close of the Reverend Evans's remarks, the members of the audience bowed their heads while he offered prayer. This ended the exercise of the day, and the visitors quietly left the house.

After all had left, the students began clearing the room and put their books and displays away.

Miss Martin gave the students some closing remarks informing them that she would be leaving the school and would probably never see many of them again. She shed a tear as she talked to each student. Now, with deepening sadness in their hearts, the students also left the building, ending the school session.

Children and visitors had all gone. Only Miss Martin remained. She had closed the windows for the final time. Now she waited at the school for a neighbor to drive her up to the Moultonborough School so she may say good-bye to Helen Peaslee, the teacher at that school. Her father would soon pick her up at that school and escort her home to Gilmanton.

Presently, the neighbor's one-horse surrey came rattling along the Coach Road and stopped in front of the schoolhouse. Miss Martin rose quickly, gathering up her few belongings, and left the school for the final time.

Presently, she boarded the wagon with her little hair trunk, which was put in the rear of the family wagon. She climbed in the wagon, and her driver clucked to the horse. With the sun low over Red Hill shining full in their faces, they followed the Coach Road along the level, and they were quickly hidden from view by the bushes lining the road.

They soon arrived at the Moultonborough School, where she would bid farewell to Helen. Then Miss Martin sat alone on the front step waiting for her father's arrival. Shortly thereafter, he drove his wagon to the front entrance. Miss Martin boarded the family wagon and sat with her father on the front seat as they retired into the west on the Coach Road.

Today, the old schoolhouse can be seen well restored on Route 25 east of Moultonborough, and it is considered one of the finest buildings in the town.

The Closing Days of the Old One-room School

For many years, the old one-room schoolhouse stood as an edifice of learning for the neighborhood in each town of the state. Time will take its toll and the old house will see its declining condition fall into disrepair. So it is for the old school on the mountain road near the Swift River. Historian J. Orville Taylor records this old school with the following:

> On the exterior of the school, we observe the general decay of the building. Notice the condition of the window-shutters after having shattered the glass by the slams of many years, have broken to many pieces. Many have fallen to the ground, while others hang by a single hinge.
>
> The clap-boards have since become loose, and many dropped one by one from their fastenings. Many of these tin boards are visible with sticking nails and loosened by the Northwest winds. Many of the boards are avenues by which the wind passes and makes the windows clatter, whistle through a knothole.

Enter the classroom—just look around and remember those early days past, and now it is time to close doors.

Remember the writing benches. They were originally sturdy planks of pinewood an inch thick. The bench was no ordinary plank, but it stood proudly, as it should, with the hacking and hewing, the scraping and borings that have inflicted the old plank and amused the youth. For more than sixty years has this old plank been subjected to the pocketknife. Accompanying the fine art that adorned the edifice are seen the innumerable writings on the

Memories remain of the old one-room school known as the Middle Neck School, circa 1900, Moultonborough, New Hampshire. *Courtesy of the Moultonborough Historical Society.*

benches, seats, walls and ceilings. Look closely, and you can see the names of girlfriends scribbled and carved on the walls and seats. Puttied windows, cracked and patched, have now been replaced by boards instead of glass. The master's desk is in fairly good condition; it stood the test of twenty years.

The floor of wide pine has seen its wear over the winter months. Brooms were not always available, and the older boys were directed to clean the floors after the traffic of wet snow was brought through the annex and classroom.

J. Orville Taylor gave an accurate description of fireplace (stove):

> *One end of the hearth has sunk an inch and a half below the floor. There are crevices between some of the tiles, into which coals of fire sometimes drop and smoke up and make the boys spring for snow. The andirons have each lost a forefoot, and the office of the important member is supplied by bricks, which had been dislodged from the chimney-top. The first shovel has acquired by accident or age a venerable stoop. The tongs can no longer be called a pair, for the lack of one of the fellow-limbs. The bar of iron, running from jamb to jamb in front, how it is bent and sinking in the middle, by the pressure of the sagging fabric above. Indeed the whole*

chimney is quite ruinous. The bricks are loose here and there in the vicinity of the fire-place; and the chimney-top has lost so much of its cement that every high wind dashes off a brick, rolling and sliding on the floor, and them tumbling to the ground, to the danger of cracking whatever heedless skull may happen in the way.

Such is the condition of the old schoolhouse, and now after many years, take a moment to reflect on the good and bad times spent in the small country school. Both parents and children have given evidence that it should be abandoned and replaced with a new structure.

For most of the students who attended the one-room district schools, there were fond memories—those years of friendship, celebration and special occasions like the teacher's birthday, Christmas party, recess play, the family presentations and the student who won the state spelling bee. Those days were the best!

6

Wisdom of Choice

Honorable Frank A. Hill, Secretary of the Massachusetts State Board of Education, offers some wise advice to those who wish to become teachers of youth. The following are excerpts of "Educational," which appeared in the *Granite Monthly* in March 1897 and was written by Fred Gowing, state superintendent of Public Instruction in New Hampshire.

If there were some way in which the State could intelligently select its own candidates for teaching the schools would fare better then they do now. Whether in deciding to become a teacher you have chosen to wisely or not, I do not know. You need in short, to train yourself for your work.

Formal education is not always the formation to become a successful teacher. Consider, what is essential to success is a matter of a happy disposition, endowment, thus, therefore, not in the power of the "Normal School" [a teachers' college] to give. Temper, scholarly power, tact, patience, ambition, moral spirit, lovable—the basis of all these elements do not necessarily come from higher education, but from ancestry and his or her environment. This present formation, and with the aid of the advanced education will give a quicker insight into the nature of education.

ACADEMIC TRAINING

First the best high school, the best teachers may give the good teacher the best equipment for success in education. A skill of good discipline, raise the child in morality and good behavior. All things may have some precious value in the skill of teaching the students.

PRINCIPLES OF TEACHING

The new candidate enters upon the general two years' course of a normal school, and the work it will aim to unfold to you should be the principles of teaching as drawn from the laws of mental activity and exemplified in the teaching experience of the world. This aim involves the study of educational psychology and educational history.

ACADEMIC KNOWLEDGE

This knowledge will aim to show how these principles may be applied in the elementary schooling. To this aim requires the following: The candidate should be most familiar with the subjects to be taught before entering into higher education. The new student of a teaching experience should consider the extent to which new energies are absorbed in conquering elementary subjects that should be mastered before admission to the student. Frank Hill reminds us that "It should start from your intelligence, not from your ignorance. I want your energies for the science and art of presentation, not for the conquest of what should already be known."

GOOD ADVICE FROM DR. C.C. ROUNDS, FORMERLY OF PLYMOUTH NORMAL SCHOOL

(Proposed in 1896)

The rural school problems seem to have always been with us, and throughout the country it remains essentially the same. Here one, attempt has been made at the solution, and there, another, but these attempts have rarely been made from any comprehensive view of the conditions essential to a complete reform. In educational conventions or discussion, it is seldom that the rural school has had directly a voice.

It is certainly my belief, as an adjunct lecturer at Plymouth State University today, that "as is the teacher, so is the school" has a large measure of truth, yet the better teachers may be handicapped by unfavorable conditions. Unfortunately, very few of the rural schools have properly trained teachers who communicate well with the young students.

Dr. Charles C. Rounds presented several facts that could provide a solution to the problem as evident during the late 1800s. His suggestions would include the following:

1. A large proportion of the teachers of rural schools cannot afford the time and expense of a two years' course in a normal school [teacher training] 2. The receipts for employment in the rural school under present conditions do not remunerate one for the expense of a normal school course. 3. Other conditions remaining the same, the attendance at a school is at an inverse ratio to the distance between school and home.

To meet these conditions, there is needed a normal training school with a short course of one-half year, the usual length of one term at the existing state normal schools.

Accordingly, deficiencies in education would be supplemented by sound teaching. Principles of teaching and of good management would be taught for the benefit of proper education of our youth. It should be remembered that from these schools would come students demanding courses of training teachers in the essentials of the youth.

Dr. Rounds recommends:

The better teacher in the rural school will call for a larger school and better conditions of organization, equipment and supervision, and all these will call for more money.

This additional burden must not be laid upon the country town. Often these towns tax themselves to sustain poor schools fourfold what the city finds necessary for its complete system. A higher tax would drive all movable capital from the town, and thus complete its ruin. We have passed from the district to the town as the smallest unit of organization and administration. The state's support must be a wider assertion of the principle that the property of the state must be held for the education of the children of the state.

According to the character of this product of our time, must the nation rise or fall. The loss and waste from failure to educate is greater, beyond all comparison greater, than these; for this loss is a failure to develop centres of spiritual forces which underlie, which organize, direct and control all else. "The average intellect of the present day is not equal to the problems presented to it." The vast majority of the people do not rise above the condition of intellectual mediocrity.

The following section was an address delivered before the American Institute of Instruction at Bethlehem in 1896 and published in *Nature and Human Nature Series* no. 1.

Helping a Teacher

By Superintendent James M. Greenwood

Note: The Kansas City, Missouri school report for 1895–96 by J.M. Greenwood, superintendent, contains much material helpful to teachers, particularly in the lines of language and primary numbers. The following letters presented to the reader from a principal to a young teacher are suggestive and helpful:

My Dear Miss: I have tried faithfully for two years to lead you to see the necessity of neat, accurate, definite work of requiring your pupils to do exactly what you ask them to do.

You do not consider these things necessary; you are not in sympathy with the spirit that dominates the highest standard of work in our schools, and fail to realize that regard to detail, and firm, quiet discipline and indispensable in cultivating attention and in developing thought.

You are ambitious and want to do good work, yet you will not see that close, sympathetic training is necessary.

You neglect the little things of life; for our lives are made up of little things. Great events seldom, if ever, enter.

What you need is to plan your work more definitely; to study the art of questioning; to believe in accuracy and discipline.

This criticism is made in the kindliest spirit. I trust you will accept it in a like spirit, and believe me truly your friend and helper.
Sincerely yours.

My Dear Miss: I wish you would ask yourself the following questions each evening this week.

At the close of the week, please let me know what you have gained by so doing.
1. Have I required my pupils to do what I have asked them to do?
2. Have they stood still and erect while reciting?
3. Have I required accurate statements from them?
4. Have they been diligent during study periods? If not, why?
5. Has the written work of the day been neat and legible?
6. At nine o'clock in the morning, was the day's work definitely planned?
7. Did I really teach and clinch something new during each recitation?
8. Have I tried to talk above the noise?
9. Have I followed my programme?
Sincerely yours.

My Dear Miss: In your general management, you fail to realize that sincerity should be the basic principle. I say this in all kindness as your friend.

I tried to believe that your first inaccurate reports were not intentional; but as I saw the same inaccuracy repeated day after day, I felt that I must speak to you. After this, to use your own language, I hope you would "profit by yesterday's lesson." But the same inaccurate reports continued. Those three children that you sent back to their seats knew they were tardy. What was the influence?

You manifest the spirit you have shown in regard to this matter at other points. Unless it is checked, it will ruin your work as a teacher, and take out of your life that quiet, restful peace which is the foundation of all true happiness.

After carefully considering the matter, I can see but one of two courses to pursue:

1. To ask for your immediate removal.

2. To try to lead you to see existing conditions in their true light, and help you to bury the past in a future devoted to the highest ideals upon the latter course.

Now my dear Miss, let me say to you that there is not anything in life which can meet with real success unless it rests upon the rock of sincerity. Other structures may stand for a while, but they soon become top-heavy and fall.

Look at this matter carefully, and in the light of judgment, and though the lesson is a hard one, one that will hurt and that deeply, yet feel and know that you can gain from it strength that will change the whole current of your life.

I trust you will accept this criticism in the spirit in which it is given, and feel that you will ever find in me a real friend and helper.

Sincerely yours.

THE SCHOOL MASTER'S EXAMINATION

The following examination is presented by the author as a satire with some humor; however, it is based on fictional rules from a school district prudential committee.

Our early schools were under very strict home rule and the teachers under even closer scrutiny, as mentioned in Chapter Two. By the New Hampshire laws on teachers of the common schools, they shall be examined in all the required disciplines of academic studies and in other branches usually taught in these common district schools.

The prudential committee of the town required that "no person shall be employed or paid for services as a teacher unless he or she shall produce and deliver the Prudential Committee a certificate of the school committee of the town, that he or she is well qualified to instruct youth in the branches to be taught."

The school committee, however, "shall without a petition, dismiss any teacher who is found by them incapable or unfit to teach, or whose services are found unprofitable to our schools, or who shall not confirm to our regulations given and prescribed by them."

A good example of the examination given the school master was one given by the Reverend Evans, Deacon Pitchpipe, Squire Roundabout and Dr. Liverleaf on the one part and the master on the other.

The dialogue went like this:

Reverend Evans to the Master: "What part of mankind are fore-ordained to be saved?"

Master: "All who conduct themselves in a Christian manner."

Deacon Pitchpipe: "How many molasses will it take to keep Thanksgiving in the whole State of New Hampshire?"

Master: "That depends on the number of pumpkin heads."

Squire Roundabout: "What is the proper way of speaking, to say I inspect or I expect?"

Master: "That depends on whether it be a matter of inspection or expectation."

Dr. Liverleaf: "Which of the western states is Filadelfa?"

Master "It is neither. It is one of the middle states."

Deacon Pitchpipe: "What denomination of Christians do the Turks belong to?"

Master: "Not any. They are Muslims."

Squire Roundabout: "How much pork will it take to support a large family?"

Master: "Upward of a considerable."

Dr. Liverleaf: "What was the name of the Spartan colonel who fought 'til he was blue at the Straits of Gibraltar?"

Master: "Leonidar fought nobly at the Straits of Thermopylae."

Reverend Evans: "What part of speech is this book?"

Master: "This book makes two parts of speech."

The master was next required to spell wine-pipe, cheeney-ware and a number of other words that the committee pronounced with equal correctness. But to make a short work of it, after the master was drilled about three and a half hours in a style equally learned, important and dignified with the above specimen, he had the impudence to turn upon his assailants, and the following counter-examination took place:

Master to Deacon Pitchpipe: "Will you be good enough to tell me what religion the pagans profess?"

Deacon Pitchpipe: "Why, I take it, sir, they are but little better, if any, than so many heathens."

Class picture of the Moultonborough School, 1934. *Courtesy of the Moultonborough Historical Society.*

Today the schools are empty and left to the care of the local historical societies and private owners. *Courtesy of the Moultonborough Historical Society.*

Master: "Squire Roundabout, supposing a frog should undertake a jump to the top of a steep ninety feet high, but as often as he hopped up two feet, he fell back three. How long would it take him to reach the top?"

Squire Roundabout: "I have not time now to calculate it, but for a rough guess, I should say upward of a fortnight."

Master: "What is your idea of 'Captain Symmes's hole'?"

Squire Roundabout: "Why it would answer no purpose at all—that 'twas so shallow a tater would all freeze before spring, and I guess he'll find it so sooner or later.

Master: "Dr. Liverleaf, what is the altitude of Boston?

Dr. Liverleaf: "Why, sir, it is sometime since I looked at my geography, but I should say, as far as my recollection serves me, about fifty degrees north."

Master: "Deacon Pitchpipe, how do you spell boot-jack?"

Deacon Pitchpipe: "B-ooo-u-t-e, boot-j-a-k, jack—boot-jack. I learnt that of Uncle Stephen, when I war'nt about knee high to his great toe."

Master: "Squire Roundabout, how do you spell puzzle?"

Squire Roundabout: "P-u-ez-l. puzzle."

Master: "What kind of a letter is an ez'l?"

Squire Roundabout: "Why sir, it is a little out of my mind just now, but I think I have seen something like it in Delwort's *Spelling Book* or Perrin's dictionary."

Master: "Deacon Pitchpipe, who was the first Christian emperor?"

Deacon Pitchpipe: "Alexander the Great, the same who first introduced the Reformation into Old England."

Master: "Dr. Liverleaf, how do you spell, Adam?"

Dr. Liverleaf: "A byself a, d, a-m, dam, Adam."

Master: "Please inform me what tree produces cork and in what region it grows?"

Dr. Liverleaf: "Yes, sir, I'll endeavor to. The tree is a corkusqueribus, and it grows in Lapland, where the Peruvian bark is brought from."

Master: "What part of speech is 'and'?"

Dr. Liverleaf: "It's a disjunctive preposition that serves to unite two paragraphs and form them into one sentence.

The master received his appointment at the East School on Vittum Hill in District Number One and performed his duties with great proficiency.

LIST OF ONE-ROOM SCHOOLHOUSES

Croydon Village School—or the Red School, a brick school in Croydon (Sullivan County)—reports to be the longest continuously operating one-room schoolhouse, in use since 1794.

The Blue School in Landaff (Grafton County) was built in 1858.

Schoolhouses That Are Closed but Preserved

North School in Kensington, in operation from 1842–1952.

Indian Stream One-Room Schoolhouse in Pittsburg, New Hampshire, in operation from 1897–1939.

Madison Corner School in Madison, in operation from 1835–1949.

District Schoolhouse No. 1 in Hooksett, in operation from 1839–1912.

Brick Schoolhouse in Sharon, in operation from 1833–1920.

District No. 5 School in East Washington, in operation from 1849–1937.

District No. 1 Schoolhouse in Nashua, in operation from 1841–1921.

Pleasant Valley School House, built in South Wolfeboro in 1805 and transported to the Clark Museum Complex in the 1950s.

High Tops School in Westmoreland, built in 1789 and remodeled extensively in 1846.

It seems most fitting to close the book with this poem of Memory and Reflection.

THE OLD DISTRICT SCHOOL

No more the school house by the road
Defies the wind and rain and snow;
No more it stands where once it sowed
The seeds of learning long ago.

No more on winter's bleakest day,
Its welcome warms some frost-chilled hand;
No more, when spring smiles fair and gay,
It chains a restless, listless band.

The sun of morning saw them come.
The moon of evening saw them go;
From home to school, from school to home.
Like tides of ocean, to and fro.

Opposite, top: Reunion at the Moultonborough Central School in 1927. *Courtesy of the Moultonborough Historical Society.*

Opposite, bottom: The Ashland Grammar School, circa 1890. The Ashland Village Graded School was built in 1877–78. Three departments were established: primary, intermediate and high grammar. All were located in four rooms. Due to increasing enrollment in the early 1900s, two rooms were made on the top floor to provide for grades one through nine. Today, classes are no longer held in the school; however, it does remain as an important landmark of the town. This picture shows a reunion of past students who proudly attended the Ashland school. I was pleased to teach in this school for one year (1980). My room was on the right of the first floor. *Courtesy of the Ashland Historical Society.*

The Lower Intervale School is seen near the intersection of Routes 3, 25 and the River Road. *Courtesy of the author.*

Midst sleepy silence wake the sounds
Of busy voices from within,
And on its weedy trodden grounds
At nooning rose a merry din.

When summer solstice comes again,
The school house slept forsaken there.
It's passed, the dog star's sultry reign;
Our harvest moon shown bright and fair.

Alas, at the school life winged away,
That aged school house died at last,
But all forlorn awhile it lay,
A relic of the fading past.

Where children's children learned to spell,
And fathers came to read and write,
The scythe of time unsparing fell
And swept the school house from man's sight.

No more that school house stands, no more
Beside the road, beside the hill;
Its work is done, its day is o'er,
Yet memory clings around it still.

Author Unknown

Appendix

SUPERVISION OF PUBLIC SCHOOLS, 1895

The following excerpts are from an address by the Honorable F.W. Dickinson, state board of education for the commonwealth of Massachusetts, which was presented before the Nashua Teachers' Club on January 27, 1895.

This material is a supplement to Chapter Two ("School District Established"), which embellishes on the fine-tuning of the proper supervision of the school system.

During the colonial days the welfare of the public student was directly provided to the care of the selectmen of the community. Those gentlemen were assisted by the clergymen of their parish and often required to perform the duties of the school administrator.

As time passed on and more academic notions of the operation and supervision of the school system began to take progressive action, the more thoughtful men of the town became dissatisfied with the limitation of the education of their youth. Their concerns were that of untrained teachers and inferior courses of instruction being offered; the schoolhouse was unfit for use.

In 1854 the legislature authorized the towns by vote to choose a school committee and superintendent of schools. Under this act ninety cities and large towns have availed themselves of its provisions. So in 1870 a law was passed allowing the towns to unite for the support and employment of school superintendent.

It was not until the act of 1888 that 146 towns had formed themselves into districts and provided special supervision for their public schools.

Some of the following results of supervision are here within this list, created by Honorable J.W. Dickinson in 1895:

1. There has been a large increase in the attendance of pupils in all grades of the public schools.
2. The teaching force has been greatly improved.
3. The schools are better graded.
4. They are supplied with better courses of study.
5. They are taught by better methods.
6. They are better equipped with text-books and other means of study and teaching.
7. New schoolhouses are constructed more in accordance with the principles of comfort, convenience, and beauty.
8. The superintendents secure a more intelligent care of schoolhouses.
9. They make arrangements for a more economical expenditure of money; in many instances saving by their intelligent use of funds more than they receive in salaries.

The state board of education recommended that a school district that has fewer than thirty schools should be allowed to receive state aid. Honorable F.W. Dickinson recommended the following:

When a union of towns has been affected, it should not be allowed to break up until after a trial of three years, unless it obtains the consent of the state superintendent of schools, or of the state board of education.

It is generally understood that the superintendent should be permitted with the approval of the committee, to determine the number of schools a town shall maintain, to nominate the teachers to be employed, to make out courses of studies for the schools, to direct the teachers in their methods of teaching, to select the text books to be used, to have charge of the janitors, and to see that the schoolhouses are in order.

Agents (committees) should be employed to visit the schools in order to ascertain the condition of school buildings and intelligently examined; that any neglect on the part of the towns to supply their schools with the means of teaching may be discovered, and that accurate information may be obtained concerning courses of studies in use and methods of teaching.

From such observations the visitors would be able to infer the preparation of the teacher to perform in a skilful manner the responsible duties of his office.

RULES AND REGULATIONS FOR THE GOVERNMENT OF THE PUBLIC SCHOOLS, 1807.

(In view of Modern Notions in School Affairs, the following Report of the City of Portsmouth, of the year, may be interesting.)

The school committee of the town of Portsmouth agreed on the following rules and regulations as the best calculated, in their opinion, to form a proper system of public education for the town:

Article I.
The hours of attendance in all the schools shall be viz., from the first of April to the first of October, from 8 o'clock a.m. to 12, and from 2 p.m. to 6 p.m.

Article II.
No boy shall be admitted into school one quarter of an hour after the bell has rung, without a written apology from his parents or guardian.

Article III.
The holiday shall include, viz., the Fast day, the Fourth of July, Thanksgiving day, Christmas day, Thursday afternoons, Saturday afternoons, and one week in each year; provided that no two schools be vacant at one time and the same time.

Article IV.
Strict discipline and good order must be maintained in all the schools. To affect which, the masters should first endeavor to operate on the scholars' minds by the sense of shame for improper conduct, and by the pride of good behavior. They are to be sparing of promises and cautious of threats, but punctual in the performance of the former study in the execution of the latter.

If neither the sense of shame nor the pride of virtue be sufficient to preserve strict obedience and attention on the part of the scholars, recourse must be had to the infliction of moderate and becoming corporal punishment, and in the last resort to temporary dismissal or to expulsion.

Article V.
The masters are enjoined to inculcate on the scholars the propriety of good behavior whilst absent from school, and to take cognizance of their conduct in the streets; particularly noticing and correcting quarrels, profane and indecent language, rudeness, insolence, and everything that militates against good manners and sound morals.

Article VI.
The masters shall cause the by-laws of the town and the regulations for the government of the schools to be read to the scholars on the morning of the first Monday in every month; and a strict observance of them is positively enjoined.

Article VII.
Schools exercises shall be introduced in the morning by prayer, and by reading a portion of the Holy Scriptures, and in the evening shall be concluded in the same manner.

Article VIII.
Every scholar shall furnish himself with such books as are required by these regulations for the class to which he shall be attached, within one week after his admission, or be dismissed from the school till he has procured them.

Article IX.
Every scholar shall be required to recite a morning lesson from such book as the master shall direct.

LATIN AND GREEK GRAMMAR SCHOOL

Article X.
The preceptor pf the Latin and Greek grammar school shall teach the rudiments of the Latin and Greek languages when required so to do; and

he is to be of classical ability to qualify scholars for admission into any of the neighboring universities. He shall also teach the English language grammatically, rhetoric, composition, elocution, geography, the use of the globes, writing in its varieties and arithmetic.

Article XI.
No child shall be admitted into the above mentioned school under ten years of age. Excepting he be designed for the study of the learned language, In which case he may be admitted at the age of eight; provided, nevertheless, that no child shall be at any age admitted into this school excepting he be able to read any English author with readiness, and to class in spelling with the lowest class in the school.

Article XII.
The books for the Latin students shall be, viz., Adam's Latin grammar, Latin primer, Cornelius Nepos, Tully's offices, Ceasar's commentaries, Cicero's oration, Virgil, Sallust, and Horace. Of the higher classics: the text in use is Clark's introduction to the making of Latin is to be used for exercises written at home and brought into school for revision and corrections every morning.

Article XIII.
The books for the Greek students shall be, viz, the Gloucester Greek grammar, the Greek testament, Exnophon's Cyropaedia and Collestanea Graeca.

Article XIV.
This school for the study of the English language and for geography, writing, and arithmetic, shall be divided into four classes, and the books for each class shall be, Viz.:
Class I. Murray's English grammar; Murray's exercises; Murray's English reader; Blair's Rhetoric abridged; Walker's dictionary abridged; Morse's geography abridged; Welsh's mercantile arithmetic. Writing, elocution, and composition are to be taught and strict attention is to be paid to orthography.
Class 2. Murray's grammar abridged; Murray's introduction to the English reader; Walker's dictionary abridged; Ticknor's exercises; Merrill's arithmetic.
Classes 3 and 4. Murray's grammar abridged; Walker's dictionary abridged; arts and sciences abridged; Pike's orthography; Merrill's

arithmetic; the Bible is to be read in all classes, and all the scholars are to be instructed in writing.

Article XV.
The number of Latin, Greek, and English scholars admissible at one and the same time shall not exceed seventy; and as in its original establishment this school was intended for classical education, if Latin and English scholars should be offered at one and the same time, and there should not be room for both agreeable to the limitation of seventy, then and in that case the Latin scholars are to have the decided preference of admission.

THE ENGLISH GRAMMAR SCHOOL

Article XVI.
The respective masters of the north central, and south English schools, and of other schools which may be established for similar purposes, shall be able to teach reading, orthography, the use of pauses, writing in its varieties, arithmetic, English grammar, and geography.

Article XVII.
No child shall be admitted into these schools unless he has attained the age of six years, and be able to read words of two syllables without spelling, and to class in the spelling book.

Article XVIII.
The north, central, and south English schools shall be divided into as many classes as may be found convenient for the best instruction of the children. The books for the several classes shall be, viz.:

For the first class. Murray's grammar; Murray's exercises; Murray's introduction to the English reader; Walker's dictionary abridged; Dwight's geography; Merrill's arithmetic.

Second class. Murray's grammar abridged; Walker's dictionary do.; arts and sciences do.; Ticknor's exercises; Merrill's arithmetic; the Bible is to be read in both these class, and writing is to be taught.

Third class. American Preceptor; Pike's Orthography; New Testament.

The lower classes. The New Testament; Pike's Orthography; writing and arithmetic are also to be taught.

REWARDS OF MERIT

Article XIX.

The rewards will be adjudged at the discretion of the committee, on the quarterly visitation days, to the scholars of the respective schools, according to the course of studies established by these regulations, viz.:

 1ˢᵗ. To the scholar who shall present to the committee the best original composition on any given subject.

 2ⁿᵈ. To that scholar who shall have committed to memory and repeated the greatest number of lines since the last quarter day.

 3ʳᵈ. To that scholar who shall have made the greatest proficiency in writing since the last quarter day.

The Center Harbor Village School was built in 1886. The deed was recorded on July 12, 1886. Originally, it was a one-room schoolhouse, the first of a more modern type to be built in the town. The picture shows a center window. In this section was the schoolmaster's desk set upon a raised platform. At a cost of $1,450.73, the schoolhouse was built by Charles Dwinell Maloon. The first day in the build was October 17, 1886. The term of instruction was ten weeks, and the enrollment was twenty-five students. In 1902, a small room was added. The school was then divided, and two teachers were employed. There was an enrollment of forty students, twenty in each room. After a few years, the small room was enlarged to its present size. Today, the schoolhouse is located on Route 25B leading up the hill toward West Center Harbor and Holderness. The edifice presently belongs to the Center Harbor Historical Society and is open to the public during the summer months. *Courtesy of the Center Harbor Historical Society.*

4th. To the head scholar in each class when the quarterly examination is finished.

None of the above rewards will be given, unless the scholar to whose lot they may fall, shall have made more than usual proficiency in his studies during the quarter.

A true copy, Th. Elwyn

Recording Secretary

Bibliography

Beckman, Jane, Patricia Heard, Shirley E. Lyons, D. Bruce Montgomery, Letitia O'Neil, Caroline Snyder and George, G. Bush. *History of New Hampshire Education*. Washington, D.C.: Government Printing Office, 1898.

Bickford, Gladys S. *Centre Harbor, New Hampshire*. Meredith, NH, Centre Harbor Historical Society, 1986.

Bisbee, Ernest E. *The White Mountain Scrap Book*. Lancaster, NH: Bisbee Press, 1946.

Blaisdell, Carl F. *Meredith Parade, Meredith, NH*. Meredith, NH: Meredith Historical Society, 1990s.

Clayton, John. "District # 5 School, East Washington, N.H." *Manchester (NH) Union Leader*, March 9, 2000.

Dickinson, Hon. F.W. "Supervision of Public Schools, Concord, NH." *Granite Monthly* 20, no. 3 (March 1896).

Farmington Historical Society. *Images of America: Farmington*. Dover, NH: Arcadia Publishing Co., 1997.

Gowing, Fred. "Rules and Regulations for the Government of the Public Schools." *Granite Monthly* 22, no. 6 (June 1897).

———. "To One Who Wishes to Become a Teacher." *Granite Monthly* 22, no. 3 (March 1897).

Greenwood, J.M. "Helping A Teacher." *Granite Monthly* 22, no. 4 (April 1897).

Heald, Bruce D. *Images of America: Around Squam Lake*. Charleston, SC: Arcadia Publishing Co., 2002.

———. *Landmarks and Legacy*. Meredith, NH: Faye's Boatyard, 1990.

————. *Meredith, NH*. Dover, NH: Arcadia Publishing Co., 1996.

————. *Reminisce the Valley*. Meredith, NH: Weirs Publishing Company, 1992.

Henretta, James A., David Brody and Lynn Domenik. *America: A Concise History*. Vol. 1, Boston/New York: Bedford/St. Martin's, 2012.

Hurd, Hamilton D. *History of Merrimack & Belknap Counties, New Hampshire*. Philadelphia, PA: J.W. Lewis & Co., 1885.

Johnson, Clifton. *The Country School*. Boston, MA: Thomas Y. Crowell & Co., 1907.

Kramer, Madison. "One-room School Houses Still in Operation in NH." *New Hampshire Magazine* (September 2013).

Leavitt, Dudley. *Complete Directions for Parsing the English Language*. Concord, NH: Jacob B. Moore, 1826.

————. *Scholar's Review and Teacher's Daily Assistant*. Portland, ME: A. Lyman & Co., 1811.

McDuffee, Franklin. *History of Rochester, New Hampshire*. Rochester, NH: J.B. Clarke Co., 1892.

Meredith Historical Society. *Early Meredith 1968*. Meredith, NH: Meredith Historical Society, 1976.

————. *Reminiscences of Meredith (from the Bicentennial)*. Meredith, NH: Meredith Historical Society, 1776.

Monoon, James. "Hints to Teachers." *Granite Monthly* 23, no. 1 (July 1897).

Pickering, Agnes N. *Meredith School History*. Meredith, NH: Meredith Historical Society 1968.

Plymouth Historical Society. *Images of America: Plymouth*. Charleston, SC: Arcadia Publishing Co., 1998.

Robinson, William F. *Abandoned New England*. New York: Little, Brown Co., 1978.

Rosal, Lorenca C. *God Save the People: A New Hampshire History*. Orford, NH: Equity Publishing Co., 1988.

Rounds, Charles C. "The Rural School Problems." *Granite Monthly* (December 1896).

Sandwich Historical Society. *Sandwich, New Hampshire 1763–1990*. Portsmouth, NH: Peter E. Randall Publisher, 1995.

Smith, Jonathan. "Recollection of a District School." *Granite Monthly* 34, no 4 (April 1903).

Squires, James D., PhD. *The Granite State of the United States*. Vol. 2. New York: American Historical Company, Inc., 1956.

Taylor, J. Orville. *The District School as It Was*. New York: J. Orville Taylor, 1838.

Wallace, William, and Marjorie Wheeler. "A Little World By Itself." *Sandwich, New Hampshire 1763–1990*. Portsmouth, NH: Sandwich Historical Society and Peter E. Randall, publisher, 1995.

Weld, Allen H. *Parsing Book*. Boston: Sanborn, Carter, and Bazin, 1856.

Index

About the Author

Bruce Heald, PhD, adjunct faculty for the History Department at Plymouth State University; associate professor at Babes-Bolyai University, Cluj-Napoca, Romania; senior purser aboard the MS *Mount Washington* (forty-eight years) and author of more than forty books and numerous articles about the history of New England.

Dr. Heald is a graduate of Boston University, University of Massachusetts–Lowell and Columbia Pacific University. He is presently a fellow in the International Biographical Association and the World Literary Academy in Cambridge, England. Dr. Heald is the 1993 recipient of the Gold Medal of Honor for literary achievement from the American Biographical Institute. From 2005 to 2008, he was a state representative to the general court of New Hampshire. Dr. Heald resides in Meredith, New Hampshire, with his family.

Visit us at
www.historypress.net
....
This title is also available as an e-book